I0390890

THE PHILOSOPHER'S TOOLBOX FOR ENTREPRENEURS

THE PHILOSOPHER'S TOOLBOX

FOR ENTREPRENEURS

MICHAEL F. BRUYN

A guide for entrepreneurs who do not read management books but would like some inspiration all the same.

for Tita

All quotations are from public sources such as
The Gutenberg Project and Wikiquote.org

Cover illustration: Michael F. Bruyn

The Philosopher's Toolbox is an imprint of
MKW Uitgevers, Leiden, The Netherlands

ISBN 9781523281343
www.michaelbruyn.com

Contents

Most entrepreneurs fail.

Daniel Kahneman

There is no such thing as a failed entrepreneur.

Nassim Nicholas Taleb

Liberty means responsibility. That is why most men dread it.

George Bernard Shaw

Preface

By means of this book, I want to offer you a concise and practical handbook for entrepreneurial thinking and acting, backed by timeless wisdom. Perhaps you already run your own business. Or possibly you are currently toying with the idea of starting one. Or maybe you are a manager who would like both company and himself to take additional risk in order to reach a specific goal. But whatever your over-all aim, you will be in a position to benefit from food for thought as provided by thinkers whose ideas have stood the test of time.

Forewarned is forearmed. You will find no new theories or concepts in this book. Rather, it offers you a selection of maxims, aphorisms and chunks of whatever condensed wisdom have been around for quite some time, though not necessarily in the world of business. Usually, business and philosophy are regarded as being mutually exclusive; I beg to differ. It goes without saying that management hypes and philosophy are worlds apart. But the core of entrepreneurship is as timeless as the ideas of the great thinkers.

So no new theory. But in its place, the facilitation of new thinking.

A word of caution. I think entrepreneurship is overrated in general. The mass standardization and monotony of many 21st century office jobs stimulate many of us to dream of starting our own businesses. Often, the risk/return equation of such ventures is viewed too optimistically. Success stories are magnified, and romanticized. The loneliness and existential insecurity that typically go with being on your own are underestimated. If you are well-educated, even-tempered, patient and generally well-liked by people, you may have a better chance of doing interesting work and making good money if you join a larger corporation. Although of course today's payroll jobs aren't what they used to be in terms of salary, benefits or job security.

So one other thing you are not going to find in this book are motivational can-do messages. If you need those, you're probably not an entrepreneur in the first place. You have or will become an entrepreneur because of a certain inevitability. If that seems to be the case, this little book may well help you to find out if it really is the right calling for you, and if so, may also help you make a much better job of it.

The book is organized into 34 chapters. Each chapter is focused on a theme which has been on entrepreneurs' minds through the ages: getting ideas, turning ideas into action, dealing with uncertainty and risk, getting and keeping customers, buying and selling, cost control, managing people, dealing with competition and so on. For each theme you will find a selection of wise sayings which are illustrative of the issues you may encounter in each area. Each saying is further illustrated by some brief observations from real business life. If you sometimes detect incongruity between different sayings, that is in order: whilst the opposite of a small truth is usually a falsehood, the opposite of a great truth is usually another great truth. That's the way it is. Good luck with your enterprise.

1 On your own

Not everybody is cut out to be an entrepreneur. If it's job security you're after, or a fairly good chance of making fairly good money, a corporate career is probably better. Or joining a reputed law firm. Or a bank. There is certainly no shame in recognizing that.
Some people say that it takes three things to become a successful entrepreneur: greed, ignorance and luck: not exactly the first things a nice, balanced, thoughtful and responsible person would identify with. Let's rephrase, then. You must have a passion for profitable results. You should not let your own intellect or the opinions of others get in the way of acting decisively. And you must be ready to deal with extreme outcomes, positive or negative. Here is what some great thinkers have to say about it.

To be a man is, precisely, to be responsible.

Antoine de Saint-Exupéry
French aristocrat, writer, poet and aviator, 1900-1944

No better way to assume responsibility than starting and

running your own business. If things go well, and also if they don't, you have no higher power to answer to but yourself, apart from maybe your family members, who have to share the burden of a wildly varying household income and of your erratic working hours. A thought as scary as it is comforting.

Something is always born of excess: great art was born of great terror, great loneliness, great inhibitions and instabilities. And it always balances them.

Anaïs Nin

Cuban-American writer, 1903-1977

Great entrepreneurs are like successful creative artists, with whom they share the qualities of ignorance and luck. As to greed, the jury isn't out. Just like an unhappy childhood may prove to be a writer's goldmine, a troubled background may well be a common characteristic of any man or woman who goes at it alone. You don't become an entrepreneur when you fit in too well.

Few great men could pass personnel.

PAUL GOODMAN

American writer, 1911-1972

Indeed, fate may have steered you to running your own show by simply putting Human Resources in your way at the time you were still a hired hand. The HR department is typically staffed by people who tend to have a low risk appetite. Their device is 'don't do the wrong thing' rather than 'do the right thing'. You are a-typical and therefore a liability. Hiring or promoting mavericks like you does not serve their own interests, as you may have found out already when applying for a corporate job or promotion. You will have been turned down by HR or by its passive influence, probably with a vague explanation including some lame talk about 'lack of team player ability'.

Why do you have to be a nonconformist like everybody else?

JAMES THURBER

American humorist and cartoonist, 1894-1961

Millions of people are dressed in the latest fashion and yet every one of them thinks that this habit underlines his or her unique personality. People the world over practice the same fashionable language, and they all like to think this makes them innovative wizards. Managers use all kind of business speak to prove their enlightenment to themselves and to others. Entrepreneurs are different. They may look unremarkable in their appearance and may not use buzzwords. But their view of the world is unique. Like the artist, they notice opportunities that others overlook and have a sense to act upon them. Acting the part rather than looking or talking it is what makes them tick.

2 The Goal

If you are smart and reflective, you will not start your own enterprise unless it is based on a distinctive idea. Perhaps you see a better way for small business owners to do their bookkeeping online. Maybe you have designed a pair of jeans that will go well with a smart sports jacket. Or, after wasting a lot of baking dough, you now have a couple of recipes for pizzas that taste like haute cuisine but can be sold at eight dollars each. And now you want to sell it to the world.

The center of every man's existence is a dream.

G.K. Chesterton
English writer, 1874-1936

We are all driven by something: ideas, wishes, ambitions, desires. In short, by something which has not yet materialized. To live is to long for something. Entrepreneurs are no exception. They usually have strong imaginative powers and can think beyond the here and now. Fueled by dreams of how things could and should be, they are ready to take on new ventures.

If you are both poet and killer, you get rich.

David Ogilvy

English advertising executive, 1911-1999

Thinking of new opportunities is only half of the job, of course. You must also act on your ideas, or else they will die. Better to kill than be killed, so know when you've finished thinking. And recognize that the best way to get new ideas is by experimenting: trial-and-error, learning-by-doing. If you're not equally strong in thinking and acting, then find people who complement you.

Regard it as just as desirable to build a chicken house as to build a cathedral.

Frank Lloyd Wright

American architect, 1867-1959

The fun of creation is a better motivator than the ambition of becoming immortal by completing immense, larger-than-life tasks. Immortality, and its more mundane cousin celebrity, should not bother you. It's decided upon by others, therefore beyond your control. And its pursuit weakens the spirit. If you want to strive for immortality all the same, you should remember that building cathedrals is complex and time-consuming. No individual involved can be more than a cog in the machine. Would you rather be a small master or a huge valet? You will find out whether your chicken house has cathedral potential in due time. Don't plan for it.

Another flaw in the human character is that everybody wants to build and nobody wants to do maintenance.

KURT VONNEGUT

American writer, 1922-2007

Having said that, many successful new businesses are not based on quantum leap inventions or jaw-dropping new designs, but on refinement or varieties of existing products and services. Innovation can be in unspectacular details which nobody has recognized so far. And staying close to the mainstream can be good business. Think of the restaurant or fashion trade, where seemingly trivial details can have a huge impact on customer satisfaction and small twists can create unique, profitable formulas. To take this even further, it requires a special business sense to leave well alone. The fashionable mantra of continuous improvement can become counterproductive. Know when to resist change. Know when it's just fine to stick to a tried and true formula. Keeping that format alive and pristine can be no small feat in itself.

Fame and power are the objects of all men. Even their partial fruition is gained by very few; and that, too, at the expense of social pleasure, health, conscience, life.

BENJAMIN DISRAELI
English politician, 1804-1881

Being an entrepreneur means that you choose to pursue your own dream rather than that of someone else. So fame, power and fortune should not, I repeat not be part of your dream. Not only because these values are indeed in short and variable supply, but also because they are controlled by the outside world and not by you.

3 Leadership

As soon as you have to show the way to employees or other people in different roles, such as customers, trade relations, politicians or other stakeholders, you will have to lead. Leading means setting a direction, creating belief and motivating people to do what they would not automatically do themselves. They may fear to enter unknown territory, fail to see personal short-term benefits or do not identify with a common goal.

It is observed that when a man is firm inside and gentle without, he is a healer. When he is hard outside and soft inside, he is useless.

AMERICAN INDIAN LEGEND

The world and especially the business arena can be a tough place. So grace under pressure is invaluable. People can put up with almost anything if it is brought to them in an understanding and gentle manner. All business leaders should possess healing ability in the sense that they are able to create comfort and confidence for the people whom they manage. Note the precise wording. Firm is better than hard and gentle is better than soft.

People in positions of power and privilege have a duty to perform at a higher level. If not them, then who?

KATHLEEN PARKER

American newspaper columnist, 1951

Whether you call the shots at a small, local PR shop or at a software company employing hundreds or thousands, people will look to you for guidance. They may well hold you up to high standards, even though they may not stick to them themselves. What's worse, they will swiftly copy your weaknesses. Whether you often arrive late at work, drive a monster truck for a car, have a drink too many every other day or bully on subordinates, these habits will be quickly adopted. Since everybody looks to you, the whole company will be permeated by bad behavior in no time. So mind the paradox: if you want to run your own show, you must be sure to set the right example at all times. In so doing, you may be required to give up a lot of personal freedom or at least some cherished habits. But this sacrifice will be well worth wile.

A return to first principles in a republic is sometimes caused by the simple virtues of one man. His good example has such an influence that the good men strive to imitate him, and the wicked are ashamed to lead a life so contrary to his example.

NICCOLÒ MACHIAVELLI

Italian political scientist, philosopher and diplomat, 1469-1527

Leading by example can be enormously rewarding. Seeing people whom you respect giving their very best, getting more out of them than they thought they had in them and maybe even converting some notorious sceptics and renegades to your cause can be highly satisfying. Loosening handbrakes and unleashing potential this way tends to be good for the business, too.

Whatever you do, you need courage. Whatever course you decide upon, there is always someone to tell you that you are wrong. There are always difficulties arising that tempt you to believe your critics are right.

RALPH WALDO EMERSON

American philosopher, essayist and poet, 1803-1882

As an entrepreneur, you should positively ignore critics, especially those who have no stake in your business. Just as you should not accept easy advice from anyone who has no skin in the game, you should not accept easy criticism either, easy here meaning free from personal consequences for the critic. Most easy criticism is based on a cocktail of envy and ignorance, reflecting the mental state of the critic rather than the subject in question.

With your supporters, it's a different matter. They do have skin in the game, because they already identify with you and therefore want you to be successful. It will rub off on them. Whether they are employees, customers or suppliers, your supporters have invested in a relationship with you. They look for ways to reap returns from that investment and to continue the development of mutual benefit. They enjoy staying employed by you, buying your company's products or trading with you. Whatever they think is worth improving is worth noting. You don't have any supporters? Then go out and develop some.

Nothing is less sincere than our mode of asking and giving advice. He who asks seems to have a deference for the opinion of his friend, while he only aims to get approval of his own and make his friend responsible for his action. And he who gives advice repays the confidence supposed to be placed in him by a seemingly disinterested zeal, while he seldom means anything by his advice but his own interest or reputation.

FRANCOIS DE LA ROCHEFOUCAULD
French writer, 1613-1680

There is one caveat, though. You 'd better be sure whom

you count as your supporters or friends, of course. And you need to be honest with yourself as well. Are you ready to accept well-intended, well-founded criticism from them? If your answer is yes, you are a rare breed. Most entrepreneurs can't or won't listen to advice. They are notoriously stubborn and self-centered. To a certain extent, they have to be.

Familiarity breeds contempt.

Aesop

ancient Greek fabulist c. 620-564 BCE

To lead is to be alone. Nowadays many entrepreneurs act as ordinary guys, wear casual clothes and behave informally with everybody around them. The fact of the matter is that they (you?) are usually decidedly egocentric and need their own space. That's why they went into business for themselves in the first place. They cannot be too close to others, lest they lose their independence of mind and action. In an atmosphere of comradery they may occasionally suggest equal footing with the people they employ, but deep down everybody knows that this is just a charade. The entrepreneur wants to keep others at bay. Fortunately, the employees want this as well. That way they can project all kinds of desires and ambitions into the business leader from a safe distance. They can bask in his charisma and his creativity without sharing the risks he is exposed to. This includes not just financial risks, but also the psychic pressure and reputational risks that go with being in charge. Think of being disgraced in the public eye, for instance, as soon as failure materializes.

There is a great man who makes every man feel small. But the real great man is the man who makes every man feel great.

G.K. CHESTERTON

Nevertheless, if you are an entrepreneur, you have the unique possibility to add new meaning to life. You may create products or services that people like because they meet previously unmet needs or needs that people were not aware of even having in the first place. You may create valuable jobs. You will be able to give your employees the idea that they are an important part of an operation which is really on to something. If you manage them well, they may develop themselves in ways they had not imagined previously possible. And finally, you may create return on investment for your shareholders. The highest reward for an entrepreneur is that he can take the world, or at least a tiny part of it, to a higher level.

4 Dealing with uncertainty and risk

Anything really worth doing is fraught with risk and uncertainty – if it weren't so, everybody would be on the case. To be an entrepreneur is not only to accept risk and uncertainty, but to actively look for it and to embrace it. It is not avoidance but clever management of them that gets results. And what is risk, anyway?

The one permanent emotion of the inferior man is fear – fear of the unknown, the complex, the inexplicable. What he wants above everything else is safety.

H. L. Mencken

American journalist, satirist and critic, 1880-1956

We all have an inclination to play it safe and now and again to long for some smooth sailing. Nothing wrong with that. But we should avoid allowing this tendency to get out of control and degrade into fear. Fear is useless. If you must fear nevertheless, fear the results of inaction.

Doubt is not a pleasant condition, but certainty is an absurd one.

VOLTAIRE

French writer and philosopher, 1694-1778

Only small minds are never subjected to doubt. So whenever you are not sure about something, you should more than anything else take this as a sign of intellectual prowess. Don't be intimidated by your own skepticism. Rather use it sensibly, and allow your mind on occasion to be rendered uncomfortable. This avoids the bigger discomfort created by wishful thinking and by the continuous drive to be sure of everyone and everything. 'Much mistaken, yet never unsure' is the classic verdict about many unsuccessful middle managers who are doomed to remain stuck in the middle for the rest of their working lives.

If I had not gone into Monty Python, I probably would have stuck to my original plan to graduate and become a chartered accountant, perhaps a barrister lawyer, and gotten a nice house in the suburbs, with a nice wife and kids, and gotten a country club membership. And then I would have killed myself.

John Cleese

English actor, comedian, writer and film producer, 1939

What entrepreneurs indeed understand, like their artistic fellowmen, is that the biggest risk in life is not to take any.

Everybody talks about how they knew the Bond films were going to be a big success, but it simply isn't true.

Sean Connery

Scottish actor, 1930

Don't be intimidated by the successes of others, by the supposedly effortless, sure-fire way this success has apparently come to them, or by those who 'knew it all along'. They most probably didn't. Hindsight makes everything look easy.

Only those who risk going too far can possibly find out how far one can go.

T.S. Eliot

American poet, dramatist, literary critic, and editor, 1888-1965

Collecting bruises is inevitable. As long as they don't leave painfully detracting scars, there is not much to it. So take a good hammering every now and then, and take it in your stride. It's the only way to find out that you have deployed your full potential.

If a nation values anything more than freedom, it will lose its freedom, and the irony of it is that if it is comfort or money that it values more, it will lose that too.

W. Somerset Maugham

English writer, 1874-1965

Compare this to companies who are paralyzed by contemporary shareholder dictates such as maximizing profitability or Economic Value Added. In their hunt for maximum profit, they risk neglecting their core competencies (read: what they are really good at) and stand to lose their competitive edge. They take on immense risks through aggressive financing, loading themselves up with debt. Likely next stage of the drama is their profitability evaporates or disappears overnight. The reasons:

lower customer ratings and lower sales, higher debt service costs or a killing cocktail of both.

If you take risks and face your fate with dignity, there is nothing you can do that makes you small; if you don't take risks, there is nothing you can do that makes you grand, nothing.

NASSIM NICHOLAS TALEB

Lebanese-American writer, trader and risk engineering scientist, 1960

There is uncertain profit, but certain honor in taking risks. Not taking any risks means that you only want to exploit what's already there. You want to benefit from risks which have been taken or are still being taken by others. This is the quality of a profiteer. No entrepreneur with a grain of self-respect could accept that.

Courage is willingness to take the risk once you know the odds. Optimistic overconfidence means you are taking the risk because you don't know the odds. It's a big difference.

DANIEL KAHNEMAN

Israeli-American psychologist, 1934

But let's not take senseless risks. Try to assess the odds

at all times. Do your homework. Don't decide about anything on a whim. Be courageous, not overconfident. There is no checklist on courage. Ask your friends, your partner or your associates how they honestly rate you. Or find a good, impartial sparring partner with no vested interest.

5 Being creative

We are not necessarily talking creativity in the narrow, classical sense, the way in which artists, novelists and other free spirits give meaning to the word. To an entrepreneur, creativity is the broad ability to combine existing ideas into profitable new ones. It can mean all kinds of humble inventions and improvements. A pizza with exotic oriental flavours; a Little Black Dress with an invisible pocket for your smart phone; accounting software with built-in alerts when financial ratios drop below par or a smarter way to organize a prospect database. In short: to cook up new, profitable solutions to existing problems or to new ones. Defined this way, creativity is the lifeblood of any entrepreneur. No creativity equals no differentiation. And no differentiation equals no existence for your venture in the long run.

One of the greatest pains to human nature is the pain of a new idea.

Walter Bagehot

English businessman, essayist and journalist, 1826-1877

The creation of something is often associated with fun. Or at least it can be. But giving birth to a new idea, and experiencing the initial response from others to it can be tough as well. People generally don't like new things. They like what is tried and safe. So whenever you come up with something new, you will meet with opposition. You may also meet with jealousy or envy. 'If this is really such a good idea, why haven't I thought of it?' lies behind many a criticism.

The reasonable man adapts himself to the world: the unreasonable one persists in trying to adapt the world to himself. Therefore all progress depends on the unreasonable man.

George Bernard Shaw
Irish playwright, critic, activist and co-founder of the London School of Economics, 1856-1950

An additional pain of new ideas is that most of them will not amount to much. So you must stay of good cheer, knowing full well that nineteen out of every twenty ideas you produce will get nowhere. Well, that is not entirely true. Ideas that won't work will ultimately bring you to one that will. Just keep at it, and meanwhile try not to listen to people who can tell you why something won't work and, once it indeed does not work, are quick to say 'I told you so'. Their criticism is useless since initially they had no confidence in the ultimately winning idea number twenty either. Be your own unreasonable self and don't mind too much what others say.

Genius is no more than childhood recaptured at will, childhood equipped now with man's physical means to express itself, and with the analytical mind that enables it to bring order into the sum of experience, involuntarily amassed.

Charles Baudelaire

French poet, critic and translator, 1821-1867

One way of hanging on to yourself and not becoming overly conditioned by the outside world is to keep your so-called inner child alive and kicking. Being childish in this sense means being free of prejudices, conventions and practical considerations. Allow yourself a regular dose of this unrestrained thinking to think up new, fresh ideas. You can apply the adult filters later on, when doing a reality check.

Rules and models destroy genius and art.

William Hazlitt

English writer, essayist and literary critic, 1778-1830

It is, however, important that you kick your creative ideas around for a while before you perform this reality check. Don't squeeze your new product suggestion into an existing matrix. Do not immediately operate a checklist on everything you think of. Maybe the matrix or checklist could itself do with some revision anyway.

Try to act in the same way when you want to foster creativity throughout your organization. There is no ISO certificate for creative thinking, or a minimum age or a minimum functional level. So encourage all of your staff to share their ideas. Set the right example by not condemning what may initially seem silly suggestions.

Chaos often breeds life, when order breeds habit.

Henry Adams

American historian, journalist, novelist and educator,1838-1918

In order for creativity to flourish, your life or your company must never be over-organized. Allow yourself regular time off. Offer your staff some time slots beyond their direct assignments to pursue whatever interests them. Give them a couple of hours each week to read, watch, reflect and discuss. Good ideas tend to pop up when there is spare time without deadlines.

6 Turning ideas into action

If your ideas won't be executed, they will die and so will your business. Unchain these ideas of yours, out of these powerpoint files and into real life.

There are those who are so scrupulously afraid of doing wrong that they seldom venture to do anything.

Luc de Clapiers, Marquis de Vauvenargues
French writer, 1715-1747

Fear of failure can paralyze a person and an enterprise alike. But especially when you have no vested interest and nothing to lose, you should not be bothered by fear of doing wrong. Look at your zero-interest situation as an opportunity to act freely. Accept that you will not achieve perfection any time. Don't bother 'what the people will say'. And if you must bother: would you like to be known as a man or woman of missed opportunities?

The greatest loss of time is delay and expectation, which depend upon the future. We let go the present, which we have in our power, and look forward to that which depends upon chance, and so relinquish a certainty for an uncertainty.

LUCIUS ANNAEUS SENECA

Roman philosopher, statesman and dramatist, c. 4 BC-A.D. 65

Procrastination is killing for every entrepreneur. Avoid the endless elaboration of grand schemes where, one fine day, based on perfect information, everything will be perfectly connected to everything else. Don't wait for the ideal market situation either. It will never materialize. Finally, don't listen to people who are adamant that 'the organization isn't ready yet.' This statement mostly reflects their own personal discomfort and lack of interest in what you're proposing.

If you keep thinking about what you want to do or what you hope will happen, you don't do it, and it won't happen.

DESIDERIUS ERASMUS OF ROTTERDAM

Dutch philosopher, humanist and theologian, 1466-1536

Don't make the mistake of mixing up what happens in your head with what happens in real life. All the excitement in your mind may go fully unnoticed in the outside world. Fantasy and reality can benefit from each other as long as you pay attention to both dimensions. Don't stay in your splendid isolation, at least not for too long.

It had long since come to my attention that people of accomplishment rarely sat back and let things happen to them. They went out and happened to things.

LEONARDO DA VINCI (ATTRIBUTED)
Italian polymath, 1452-1519

Here is another reason to go out and act: it creates new opportunities. You will meet new people who might see opportunities for your business that you had not spotted yourself. They may lead you to other contacts, which unlocks the well-known potential of 'weak ties', the friend-of-a-friend effect. If your thinking and your personality resonates with them, such contacts might even want to solicit your support for their own activities. You might find ways to cooperate. In other words, go out and create circumstances in which good, unplanned-for things can happen to you and to your business.

7 Trial and Error

The path to success is rarely a straight line. The world is too chaotic a place for that, with too many variables beyond our control. Don't be too hard on yourself. Look at how invincible large corporations and household names frequently lose their leadership, miss the boat with new technologies or make products of wildly varying quality and market success. Mistakes and failures are unavoidable. Learn from them and make the experience as short-lived as possible.

From the end spring new beginnings.

Gaius Plinius Secundus
ancient Roman author and natural philosopher, 23-79

There is no such thing as permanent failure unless you make it so. Just reflect upon the great breakthroughs in pharmaceuticals such as penicillin which were discovered by chance while the scientists in question were fruitlessly researching another unrelated subject. Or think about the unprecedented, unexpected take-off of economies such as Germany and South Korea after WW2.

While one person hesitates because he feels inferior, the other is busy making mistakes and becoming superior.

Henry C. Link
American psychologist, 1889-1952

Don't be intimidated by failure. Don't draw yourself into a state of resignation, fretting about what might have been. Instead, try to be of good cheer. For an entrepreneur, there is no such thing as back to square one. You will have learnt from your failures. As an entrepreneur you are akin to a writer. Nothing in your life is useless. It's all grist to your mill, as long as you don't stop reinventing yourself.

Trust your own instinct. Your mistakes might as well be your own, instead of someone else's.

Samuel 'Billy' Wilder
Austro-Hungarian born American filmmaker, 1906-2002

This should be a liberating idea. In this life, nobody knows anything for sure. And nobody is infallible. We all muddle through and each of us inevitably makes a fair deal of mistakes. It is better to look at mistakes as something you are entitled to. See them as a kind of allowance, a full tank, or an opening balance of frequent flyer miles which everybody, including you, can fall back on. On such a program, available to all of us, there are different levels of perks that come with different jobs. Civil servants or bankers are rated Bronze members; managers with skin in the game get Silver; scientists, artists and entrepreneurs are entitled to Gold Card status. Let's agree that the latter may fail a little bit more often or a little more spectacularly before their goodwill balance is depleted.

If at first you don't succeed, try, try again. Then quit.
There's no point in being a damn fool about it.

W. C. Fields

born William Claude Dukenfield, American actor and comedian, 1880-1946

Though hard to put into a checklist or matrix, one of the key qualities of an entrepreneur is knowing when to throw in the towel; not too soon and not too late. In case you don't trust your own judgment, again try your supporters. If they believe in what you're working on, carry on. If they suggest changes, pay attention. If they politely suggest you change direction, pay attention even more. Remember: be sure they are genuine supporters; not people who project their personal experiences or frustrations on you, with no genuine concern for you or your company.

8 Financing the business

Though the amount may vary, every business needs capital. You need to have access to money equal to three to six months' worth of running expenses at the very least, and that is when there are already products being produced and paying customers. If you have not reached that point yet, this period may well be extended to one or two years, plus of course the investments in development and production needed for your product or service to become saleable in the first place. Where is this money going to come from?

Poverty without debt is independence.

Arabic

Whether it is through capital from equity investors or a loan from a bank or other party, to obtain funding via someone else's money means that to a certain degree you give up independence. That is not to say that you should avoid attracting money categorically; just be aware of the basic principle. Nobody will throw money at you without demanding some kind of control in return. The longer you can keep yourself from tapping other people's cash, the more you can build your business without interference. If you're not turbocharged by third party funding the path may be slower, of course. But you will experience less pressure from the outside world. And you will avoid being influenced by impatient financiers and overspending on a plan which may need resetting anyway.

Capital that seeks growth before profits is bad capital.

CLAYTON M. CHRISTENSEN

American organizational theorist and innovation expert, 1952

Remember the unpredictability of the world, and the need to proceed by trial and error? Make sure that your errors do not become too expensive and leave you with debts to settle long after the original plans have been abandoned or restructured. To use an analogy: avoid financing lavish four-figure wedding parties with today's divorce rate around fifty percent. Even more important, avoid repayment of bank loans well after the marriage itself is over. Instead of throwing a big champagne-fueled event just after rings and vows are exchanged, think of celebrating your being together in the future instead. As both a reward and an incentive to keep up the good work, you could plan to celebrate a little more lavishly after every additional five years of having been able to stick together. By the same token, you could slowly but surely build up your capital investments in the growth of the business with the help of its gradually increasing proceeds.

When prosperity comes, do not use all of it.

Confucius

Chinese social philosopher, 551 B.C.-479 B.C.

Good for you if the business does well. People stand in line to be admitted to a table at your Precious Pizza restaurant. They buy your Little Black Dress in droves. They recommend your BeanCounterz accounting software to all their friends. But try to resist the temptation of thinking that this situation is permanent. Restaurants get out of fashion for no good reason; your must-have dress may suddenly lose its edge or your software gets beaten by a new app from some teenage guys ten thousand miles away. Even a successful business is a risky business and you should deal with its finances accordingly. Plough your profits back into new product development, put money to work in totally unrelated assets or keep a nice cash cushion just in case. And pay back your debts. Whatever you do, resist the temptation to extrapolate sales curves until they break the ceiling of the graph somewhere on the upper right.

Never invest your money in anything that eats or needs repainting.

BILLY ROSE

born William Samuel Rosenberg, American impresario, theatrical showman and lyricist, 1899-1966

Don't fool yourself. Unless it is your profession, real estate is no investment for you to be in. You probably have a good deal of assets allocated in property through your private home already. Thus you do not want to increase your dependence on real estate any further by, for example, buying your office space with your excess cash. Real estate is illiquid and if it is to produce returns anywhere near the ratios of your business, it is also highly speculative. A potentially lethal combination.

Mere parsimony is not economy. Expense, and great expense, may be an essential part in true economy.

EDMUND BURKE

Irish political philosopher and politician, 1729-1797

This is not to say that you should not invest in developing the business. Just be sure that your expansion is well-considered and does not come with a worsening of your risk/return equation. That is to say more additional risk for less additional profit. Growth at lower margins, also known as buying turnover, is as hazardous as growing at a higher leverage ratio. This is where an ever higher proportion of credit money is used which increases interest payments and moreover, puts the bank effectively in charge of your company.

Most bankers dwell in marble halls,
Which they get to dwell in because they encourage deposits and discourage withdrawals,
And particularly because they all observe one rule which woe betides the banker who fails to heed it,
Which is you must never lend any money to anybody unless they don't need it.

OGDEN NASH
American poet, 1902-1971

Unless your business is firmly established with a proven product and a large, reliable customer base, chances are slim that a bank will lend you money. And if it finally does, their interests differ sharply from yours. The maximum upside for a bank is that they will get the money back they lent you earlier, plus a few percentage points mark-up. Maybe if all goes well they may provide you with a bigger line of credit down the road. But they won't share in the extreme positive or negative outcomes of your business. This is unless you go bankrupt, in which case they may not get their money back. This is not an entrepreneurial risk spectrum and indeed, banks do not like entrepreneurs. They prefer large, boring, stable corporations with large, boring, stable or steadily growing turnover and profitability figures which ensure that they get their money back.

Battered by the financial crisis as it emerged during the first decade of this century and often bailed out by the government, banks have further lowered their risk appetite. Every five-figure or six-figure credit application is subject to a tedious decision making process involving some kind of committee full of people you will never get to know. Contemporary banking employees resemble civil servants, only with a better suit, a better salary and a company car. They usually have zero independent entrepreneurial experience. They may not have worked in business at all, let alone for themselves. They are certainly not appointed to take personal risks together with you. So no matter how comradely your local bank manager acts, his understanding of you is moderate at best, his interests are aligned with yours only to a limited extent and he has no authorization to make decisions on your case.

To sum up: banks are probably not a party you as an entrepreneur could, or should, rely on. You should at least be aware of the differences as to their incentives vis-à-vis your own and avoid any erroneous 'partners in business' mirages.

Money often costs too much.

Ralph Waldo Emerson

If banks are out of the question, you must either finance the business yourself or find other lenders or equity investors. Be very cautious about whom you solicit for share capital and even more than for credit. Especially if you have to give away a majority stake and decision-making power. Never engage yourself with people who you don't like at first glance. Never work with parties or individuals of doubtful reputation. Don't get involved with people who don't seem to care about your company, its products or its people. Always ask yourself: if I myself had the cash available they are ready to throw in, would I still want them on board, because they can greatly contribute to me and my business? Don't make the mistake of thinking that 'it's only the money' they bring to the table. It never is.

9 Managing yourself

Time to talk about your most important and reliable asset. Yes, indeed, that's you. Even if it comes to managing others, put yourself first. If you are not firing on all cylinders, it is impossible to motivate, lead and monitor other people. So how do you keep yourself smart, sharp, energetic, and cheerful?

Humility does not mean thinking less of yourself than of other people, nor does it mean having a low opinion of your own gifts. It means freedom from thinking about yourself at all.

WILLIAM TEMPLE

English archbishop, 1881-1944

Although most entrepreneurs have a healthy ego, they are also quite capable of putting it aside. They take their company seriously, if not themselves. Put differently, they have no ambition to become a celebrity no matter what. They want their business to do well and are confident that when this happens, they will also be doing well. Their venture makes them forget themselves – at least a couple of times a day.

Neither blame or praise yourself.

PLUTARCH

Greek historian, biographer and essayist, ca. 46 - 127

Not thinking about yourself too much is the best way to avoid continuous, useless introspection and paralyzing self-rating. You are who you are. Avoid creating your own personal, depressing, omnipresent 'central scrutinizer' which hovers above you at all times of morning, noon and night. All the time you spend contemplating how terribly or how greatly you have performed is time diverted from attending to your company. Your supporters will not blame or praise you either. They will sometimes engage in constructive criticism which can zoom in on possible improvements. At other times they will show you that they're fond of you. And that's quite sufficient.

Not being able to govern events, I govern myself.

MICHEL EYQUEM DE MONTAIGNE

French philosopher and essayist, 1533-1592

Here's a paradox to chew on. If you want to manage yourself, you must first of all realize what is beyond your control. If you fail to do so, you run the risk of carrying the weight of the world upon your shoulders. Noble as this may seem, it is not a good idea. It will inevitably lead to overload. There are too many things which would be wonderful to influence, where it won't be possible. The earlier you grasp this, the better.

Beware the barrenness of a busy life.

SOCRATES

ancient Greek philosopher, c. 470 BC-399 BC

You actually lose things when you work too hard. Things like good cheer, the ability to put things in perspective and the power to observe and analyze. Your playfulness and hence your creativity may suffer too, as may your relations with other people. You will be less patient with them and less understanding than they deserve. Before long, your hard work turns into their problem as much as yours.

One of the symptoms of approaching nervous breakdown is the belief that one's work is terribly important.

BERTRAND RUSSELL

British philosopher, mathematician, historian, writer, social critic and political activist, 1872-1970

If you consider yourself the midpoint of the universe, and take yourself too seriously, you will make a martyr out of yourself. And martyrs, it must be remembered, tend to get burnt. Others, be they employees, business relations, friends or family, will not honor your lone soldiering at all. They will feel cornered or undervalued. If they have a healthy self-preservation mode, they will avoid or neglect you as much as possible. Or else quit. Or even burn out themselves. If you're a hard player, you will react to all this with even more hypochondria and hard work. The end of this road isn't hard to predict and it isn't happy.

Most of us spend too much time on the last twenty-four hours and too little on the last six thousand years.

Will Durant

American historian, philosopher and writer, 1885-1981

Continuously adapting to the latest events makes you manic and restless. Ultimately it wears you out. If you only pay attention to the here and now, you will be condemned to the reactive mode forever. Your thinking and doing will be limited to reflex responses to one new impulse after another. You will not be able to look back and recognize patterns, to extrapolate and to spot long term trends. You will not be able to use what others before you have found out. You won't be able to come up with anything very original either. Finally, you will probably overreact to everything and everybody. Such a mental make-up is endemic in, for example, the world of day traders in the financial markets. There, the results are dismal. It is a well-established fact that in the long run, a large majority of active security traders loses money.

Some people will never learn anything, for this reason, because they understand everything too soon.

Alexander Pope
English poet, 1688-1744

This classic piece of wisdom is sustained by contemporary research conducted by Daniel Kahneman and others. Quick intuition, and thus quick response, is not always equally reliable and useful. People tend to be over-confident about their snap judgments. Slow thinking has its own qualities. Without a certain tranquility of mind, however, you won't be able to put it into practice. This is one more reason not to overload yourself with too much stress and assumed urgent matters that supposedly demand decision-making on the spot.

We should not be exasperated by trifling and paltry incidents.

LUCIUS ANNAEUS SENECA

If you're running your own business there is always more to do than is possible. It's a big market out there and time and resources are always limited. It is thus extremely important to set the right priorities and not to fritter your days away on small stuff. There's always something to be annoyed about, be it clumsy staff, an unreasonable customer, traffic jams, erratic computers or whatever. None of these can be avoided. Don't let it get to you.

10 Dealing with people

Running a business means that you have to deal with lots of different people with lots of different agendas. What they all have in common, ideally speaking, is that they have the potential to bring you some kind of mutual, tangible benefit. Your first concern should be how each and every one of them can contribute to your company's well-being. Will they help you invent, produce or sell great products? Will they buy from you? Will they play a role in the financing of your operations? Will they introduce you to interesting persons or networks? And so on. The second question, equally important but less obvious and often neglected is what's in it for them? What do you have to offer? And does this match with what they actually want? What is it? Is it money? Honor? Credentials? Job satisfaction? A sense of purpose? New contacts? Fun?

Who treats people like pawns will soon find the chessboard empty.

Confucius

Many entrepreneurs are so fond of themselves and of their company that they think others will be happy to support them more or less unselfishly. Or at least without a balanced return of favors. If you happen to have charisma, this may work in the short run and with some people. But in the end, everybody is in business for himself. Odd as it may seem, understanding the other guy and appreciating his motives and interests doesn't come easy to many healthy entrepreneurial egos. But it is essential all the same. If you don't master this skill, you will be condemned to rotate your network continuously, replacing time and time again people who have become, well, fed up with you. You will not be able to relate longer term with other than second rate talent.

The world belongs to people with IQs of 120. Anything much greater or less amounts to a liability.

Rick Bayan

American author, 1950

Whether or not this is a problem for you firstly depends on whether or not your own IQ is in this range. If it is, you are basically well-equipped, smart enough to analyze situations, to reason effectively, and particularly to know when you have to stop thinking. You're also smart enough to understand people who are more intelligent than you are and you will know how to treat them to your mutual benefit. If your intelligence is sharply below this level, well, you would not be reading this book. If it is higher, you must be careful. Be patient with others who might come to conclusions some time after you have reached them. Also, be wary of your brilliance developing a life of its own, not leading to any tangible decisions, ever less to actions that take you or your business forward. Don't over-rely on your intelligence as a success factor either. As long-term research projects suggest, a high IQ is of limited importance when it comes to accomplishment and happiness in life.

Independence? That's middle class blasphemy. We are all dependent on one another, every soul of us on earth.

George Bernard Shaw

Not only should you be past setting yourself apart from others, but you should be willing to actively involve yourself with them. Great personal resources such as intellect, creativity, charm, or empathy impose an obligation on the possessor to share them with the outside world to the benefit of both sender and recipient. Without such sharing, an atrophy of these resources is inevitable. It's a question of use them or lose them. Also, truly great minds are fully aware of where they are weak. Nobody is equally good at everything. We all need others.

We should be too big to take offense and too noble to give it.

Abraham Lincoln

American president, 1809-1865

Getting along with other people is key to entrepreneurial success. An essential element of smooth interaction is a certain benevolence. Of course, this must be a two-way affair. Tit-for-tat is the way to go about it, with you setting the right example in the beginning and maybe allowing for one or two slips from your counterpart.

My father believed in toughness, honesty, politeness and being on time; all very important lessons.

Roger Moore

English actor, 1927

This is another way of stating the importance of being soft on people, while still being hard on the case. People can put up with almost any request, opinion, new fact or event, depending on how the information is communicated to them. Keywords are respect and understanding, clichés which rightly never go out of fashion.

Your wit makes others witty.

CATHERINE THE GREAT

Empress of Russia, 1729-1796

A sense of humor is contagious. As soon as people associate you with having a good time, they look forward to the next transaction with you. It is actually a form of leadership. You are encouraging people to unlock their own sense of humor, feeling free to be as they are, which they might feel insecure about without the right impulse.

The greatest compliment that was ever paid me was when one asked what I thought, and attended to my answer.

HENRY DAVID THOREAU

American writer and philosopher, 1817-1862

Listening is an art. For many entrepreneurs, though, this art does not come naturally. Obsessed with their venture and brimming with their own ideas, they typically find it hard to take a break and listen to what the other person has to say. And even if they solicit advice, they have a tendency to cut their counterpart short and formulate the reply which was already boiling in their own brain. No need to say that this not only violates the basic rules of politeness; it also leaves potentially valuable ideas and alternative viewpoints unnoticed.

I am a part of all that I have met.

ALFRED, LORD TENNYSON
English poet, 1809-1892

As even the healthiest entrepreneurial ego must admit sooner or later, not only are we all connected, we are also shaped by our interaction with others. Many if not most of our ideas are influenced by the world around us, as even great artists are ready to admit. For anybody running a business it is even a prerequisite. You want to make goods or services that must be sold! You cannot pull this off without your feet firmly on the ground in the world of today; this means absorbing what makes people tick and sharing knowledge and ideas with them. It's not just about market research. It's also about getting relevant ideas about what business and what products to focus on in the first place. It is what makes your creativity relevant.

If you lend someone $20, and never see that person again, it was probably worth it.

ANONYMOUS

Of course, you must always be careful to associate with the right people. Here too, you cannot avoid making mistakes. The trick, as always, is to make them in a hurry. A nice illustration of this principle can be seen at work in smart ventures who offer new hires the option to quit any time they like, with an accompanying incentive if they decide to do so. During the next couple of months, they say, we'll pay you a tidy exit sum of, say, a thousand dollars whenever you leave the company. This way, at relatively moderate cost, an effective self-regulation develops. People who want to do their best at a great company, with good opportunities for advancement, won't be tempted by such an offer. Those who will are not the type of staff the company wants to employ in the first place. For a small amount, and without much effort, you have automatically arranged separation of the wheat from the chaff.

It's no good trying to keep up old friendships. It's painful for both sides. The fact is, one grows out of people, and the only thing is to face it.

W. Somerset Maugham

Even relations with the right people do not last forever. And what goes for friendships goes for business contacts to an even higher extent because here the 'old time's sake' factor counts for less. The art of letting go is therefore very important. You must not fear to disentangle yourself from people who don't add value any longer. This value can of course be defined in a broad way: productive work, access to new customers, great ideas, interesting new introductions or whatever you consider worth wile. By the same token, you should not feel offended when you don't amount to so much anymore to people with whom you have reached great results in earlier times. The trick is not to take things too personally: who says it's about you? And look at it this way: every minute you spend on relations which have effectively reached the end of the line is deducted from limited, precious time that should be made available to valuable, promising new contacts.

Pride does not wish to owe and vanity does not wish to pay.

Rochefoucauld

The way to ensure a healthy evolution of your business relationships is to have a balanced book of favors with each of them at any moment in time. If you owe somebody something make up for it as soon as you can. Don't structurally underpay your employees or overcharge your customers. Don't over-invest time and resources in any relation, or have others over-invest in you. In fact, treat everybody the way you would treat them if you knew you would have only one week left to settle scores fairly and squarely. Having balanced books at all times is a great way by which to judge any contact by its genuine merits and to be judged accordingly yourself. You avoid that contacts muddle through for counterproductive reasons like guilt, idealization, the desire to get even or other power play. That's great stuff for novels and kitchen sink dramas, but not for business.

11 Trust

Without trust, there can be no meaningful relationship with anybody. Building it is a tedious matter which may well take years; losing it can be a matter of seconds. Without trust, people will not finance your business, grant you one minute of credit, choose you as an employer or buy your products.

We are inclined to believe those whom we do not know because they have never deceived us.

SAMUEL JOHNSON

English poet, essayist, moralist, literary critic, biographer, editor and lexicographer, 1709-1784

Don't be too quick throwing your trust to strangers, no matter how favorable your first impression of them may be. Whether it's a potential supplier, employee or customer, ask for references and follow up on them. Don't let your dissatisfaction with your current set of contacts make you susceptible to wishful thinking, projection and hasty selection. If possible, build your commitment step-by-step through short-term contracts, smaller initial assignments and the like. A sobering thought: at some point in the future, your new acquaintances may also disappoint.

One of the common failings among honorable people is a failure to appreciate how thoroughly dishonorable some other people can be, and how dangerous it is to trust them.

THOMAS SOWELL

American economist and political commentator, 1930

If you have a fine character and don't overdo it on the seven deadly sins or other breaches of commonly accepted social contracts, it is imperative for you to realize that there are plenty of people in this world who have no such inhibitions. As many a judge or psychiatrist can tell you, it is a sad fact that there are plenty of such individuals around. There is no fireproof way to avoid them. But there is a simple way to make them reveal themselves sooner rather than later. Have them talk about themselves and their affairs rather than about you. Listen very carefully how they talk about others. Do they ever praise anybody or display any indebtedness? And if so, do they only talk about how useful these people have been to them, or have they returned favors too? Do they make a lot of disparaging remarks about others? Do they blame others for projects that went wrong? Do they relish how they got the better of other people with clever scheming? These are interesting indicators and are predictive as to how they will ultimately treat *you*.

All charming people have something to conceal, usually their total dependence on the appreciation of others.

CYRIL CONNOLLY

English author, editor and critic, 1903-1974

A key problem when dealing with dishonorable people is that they may be very able to hide this from you, at least for a while. Their less agreeable side is often hidden behind a charming, trustworthy façade which they have carefully constructed over the years to cover their deficits. You may compare this to junk food or carbonated sugary water which is cunningly branded and promoted to cover the poor quality of the basic content. The best remedy is to develop an immunity to empty charm. The most pleasant way to achieve this is by becoming more endearing yourself so that you will be less intimidated by charm when others use it. Just be sure to use your charm sparingly, as a flavor rather than as a prime component of your personality. As a pinch of sugar in an excellent cappuccino, so to speak.

I'm not upset that you lied to me, I'm upset that from now on I can't believe you.

FRIEDRICH NIETZSCHE

German philosopher, 1844-1900

Avoid lying at all times. The possible benefits of a lie, if any, are outweighed by the irreversible damage which the ensuing loss of trust will do to you. Your reputation will be harmed. You will lose friends. Even worse, unless you happen to be a sociopath, you will be plagued ever after by a bad conscience and you will also lose your self-esteem. Whenever you feel that telling the truth about a person, a situation, or a personal view of yours is inappropriate for whatever reason, keep your mouth shut or, if pressed, say you can't comment. Or that you don't know. Or that you simply don't have an opinion.

12 Hiring staff

Getting the right people on board is one of the key success factors for any business. That's easier said than done, though, especially if your outfit is in its infancy and cannot offer big salaries, nice perks or much job security. If you want to attract quality staff, what do you have to offer? Be prepared to throw in lots of things which don't cost a fortune but are invaluable to good people. These include a hopefully inspiring working climate, flexible hours, your genuine personal interest in their development. And as much job responsibilities and freedom as they can take. And maybe even a little bit more than they can, because you never know what is enough until you know what's more than enough. The bad news: these conditions are actually less easy to offer in practice than plain money and may cause the occasional managerial headache. But they are essential if you want to attract and keep talent. So prepare yourself for a bumpy ride.

I don't like that man; I must get to know him better.

Abraham Lincoln

Since your business will need a lot of different talents

and resources which you probably do not all possess yourself you should be prepared to deal with people who have abilities, interests and, most probably, personalities which are also different from yours. Sometimes you may not even immediately like them. But if you want more than a group of sycophants or copies of yourself, you should be ready to allow for this heterogeneity. Don't look for clones on autopilot. Know which qualities you consider crucial for anyone employed at your company, intelligence, honesty and basic interpersonal skills for example, and allow for plenty of variety on other dimensions.

The apparent insufficiency of every individual to his own happiness or safety compels us to seek from one another assistance and support. The necessity of joint efforts for the execution of any great or extensive design, the variety of powers disseminated in the species, and the proportion between the defects and excellences of different persons demand an interchange of help and communication of intelligence, and, by frequent reciprocations of beneficence, unite mankind in society and friendship.

Samuel Johnson

It's a sign of a healthy ego when you regularly encounter people whom you honestly admire for skills or levels of skill that you know you don't possess yourself. Entrepreneurs tend to be generalists, which means that they are quite good, rather than excellent, at an impressive range of skills: creating, managing, financing, selling. It is unlikely, however, that they are world class in all or even any of these areas. In that respect, they tend to resemble senior general managers at larger companies who, as genuine generalists, are able to delegate well. But here's the catch. Contrary to these corporate managers, entrepreneurs also tend to be do-it-yourself types. If they must delegate, which they rather wouldn't, they tend to micromanage. Not because this improves results, but because they have the innate drive to do so. They started their own business because they wanted to be in control plain and simple. It thus imposes a special challenge for them to appreciate when others outdo them and which tasks are better to let others have a go at. When hiring, their inability to acknowledge their own weakness in this respect will probably radiate from the start, at the very first job interview. Talented people who sense this will quickly feel gently forced into submission and will equally quickly move on to other job openings.

If each of us hires people who are smaller than we are, we shall become a company of dwarfs. But if each of us hires people who are bigger than we are, we shall become a company of giants.

David Ogilvy

It all boils down to one simple question: do you want to

make yourself immortal, or rather your company and its products? Do yourself (and others) a favor and select the last option. Ironically, your own immortality might just benefit from it as a by-product.

Certification from one source or another seems to be the most important thing to people all over the world. A piece of paper from a school that says you're smart, a pat on the head from your parents that says you're good or some reinforcement from your peers that makes you think what you're doing is worthwhile. People are just waiting around to get certified.

FRANK ZAPPA

American musician, composer and satirist, 1940-1993

When recruiting, you should have the courage to screen the applicant and his resumé beyond all kinds of standardized criteria like the right schools, the right well-known employers and the right politically correct interests (sports, philanthropy and the like). When talking to an applicant, try to find out what else he has been up to, off the beaten track. Any endeavor which your candidate has undertaken on his own, or at least without peer pressure, is an indicator of a strong mind. Has he lived in a foreign city, earning his living as a taxi driver? Has he written poetry? Has he studied the Czech language or restored an Alfa Giulia to its former uncorroded glory? Has he already set up his first own business and failed miserably? These additional experiences are what you are looking for in any vibrant enterprise, next to academic qualifications which, as one seasoned head-hunter puts it, need not be a disadvantage.

13 Managing staff

There is truth to the saying that a company's main assets leave the building every night. But there is also truth to the famous Chinese curse wishing you lots of personnel. Be that as it may, even the greatest proprietary technology in the world cannot be turned into a profit without it being handled by people. Who else will upgrade, test, produce, sell, deliver, finance and administrate the whole thing?

All government – indeed, every human benefit and enjoyment, every virtue and every prudent act – is founded on compromise and barter.

EDMUND BURKE

No matter how good the relationship with your staff happens to be, the alignment of your interest and theirs is limited by definition. You like them to produce as much as possible at low pay and without profit-sharing, without ever taking any holidays or sick leave, while cheerfully whistling all day long and working overtime voluntarily without extra money, and of course on super-flexible contracts. They like to make as much money as possible and with maximum job security. All this is only human. Every arrangement between you and your employee is therefore based on negotiation and settlement. Neither party will ever fully get what he wants, not even in the most enlightened of companies with the most highly motivated staff. Once both sides of the table recognize this, there is nevertheless room for mutual benefits to be unlocked. More on that in the chapter about negotiation.

Masters and servants are both tyrannical; but the masters are the more dependent of the two.

George Bernard Shaw

Not only are you in a continuous trading position with your employees; like it or not, there is also a game of power between you. You are able to fire them and cut off valuables such as income, status, career progress and self-fulfillment. They, in turn, are able to quit and, if they are key to your company, may cut you or your business from much of the same. In this power game, which party has the upper hand depends on the economy, on the industry you're in, on the shape of your business and on your employee's talent. Your staff members have a strong bargaining position if they do good work, and more so if they are an essential, visible part of the service delivery as perceived by the customer such as in management consultancy or other highly personal services. If these services also have low switching barriers for clients and low entry barriers for competitors, the power balance is tilted in the employees' favor even more. The same situation can exist when employees have craftsman's skills which are not easily transferred. Not much can be done about all this. In short, choose your industry and business model carefully and know what you're letting yourself into when it comes to staffing.

If you are the boss, it's wise to remember that there are lots of things you don't know and lots of people who hope you won't find out.

MICHAEL JOSEPHSON

American speaker and lecturer, former law professor and attorney, 1942

The strongest weapon an employee has in the battle of power is knowledge - or rather your lack of it. This of course includes knowledge of what data or materials to find where, knowledge of customer details, knowledge of procedures. And, of course, knowledge of troubles ahead or already materializing. There is no golden rule to reduce this knowledge gap. Your best bet is to play it fair with everybody all the time, not to exploit or bully your workers and to avoid a reputation of dealing badly with bad news. This will reduce your staff's tendency to keep their mouth shut when it is in your interest that they shouldn't.

People who enjoy meetings should not be in charge of anything.

THOMAS SOWELL

A company which has a culture of back-to-back meetings all day, with lots of these sessions taking place on a fixed schedule, allows mediocre, clueless people to dominate the scene. It also kills valuable qualities like originality, creativity, individual responsibility and the power to act. There is one flamboyant CEO of a listed company who understands this well. As a rule, he only discusses with his other executives while standing, hardly ever when sitting down around some conference table. That way, he ensures that the exchange is as short and sweet as possible.

If you really do have to meet to engage in an extensive discussion, good preparation by everyone attending is essential. Yet this preparation almost never takes place. Think of all these board sessions you've been at where the participants ripped open the envelopes containing the necessary papers only after they'd taken their seat. One executive, aware of human nature and knowing full well how swamped everybody tends to be with paperwork, always starts meetings with a time slot which allows participants to first (re-)read the documents that are about to be discussed.

I like to praise and reward loudly, to blame quietly.

Catherine the Great

Whenever you do compliment somebody, do so for everyone to hear. Your object of celebration will feel all the more honored. The effect of setting the right example with other staff will be maximized. And you avoid the impression of playing backroom politics, also with the object of your praise (why must I be praised in secret? Does he really mean it or is he just trying to manipulate me?). On the other hand, if you have to correct someone, do so in private in order to avoid humiliation. Also, adjust your tonality accordingly. Avoid raising your voice or appearing indignant. Reasonable, professional people who make mistakes are bothered enough already by their occurrence and therefore keen enough to learn from them and avoid them in the future. Patronizing or dishonoring them is counterproductive. If they happen not to be reasonable and professional, well, you should not have hired them in the first place. Rather re-evaluate your selection procedure.

Even worse than blaming someone in public is the announcement to the object of your criticism in the presence of others that 'you want to have a word' or similar threatening speak. These others will be quick to infer that the colleague in question must have failed miserably and will let their imagination run wild as to both the crime and the punishment at hand.

You're no good unless you are a good assistant; and if you are, you're too good to be an assistant.

MARTIN H. FISCHER

German-born American physician and author, 1879-1962

Talented people want perspectives of professional and personal growth. This means that you have to make them so good, you will have difficulty in keeping them employed. They may outgrow you. Or they may get an offer they can't refuse from elsewhere. There is not much point in denying that good people stand a high chance of leaving you sooner or later. If you do deny this option and fail to cultivate them, they will still leave you, but probably after having made a less productive contribution.

14 Partnering

Though you became an entrepreneur because you wanted to run your own show, chances are that you need other skills which are not only complementary to yours but also of no less importance. If that is the case, partnering may be an option. There are several good reasons to venture into it. It can be in place of just hiring more staff. Or maybe the people you need for the business to prosper are too senior to report to you, or too expensive to employ at the full, fixed salary they would command, or too costly to hire as a consultant on an hourly basis. Maybe you just feel too lonely as sole proprietor and would welcome more sparring when it comes to getting ideas or making key decisions. In all of these cases you'd better associate with others on an equal level, which includes offering them a say in the company's course as well as a piece of the action. If all goes well, the business will grow as a result and you and your partners will each have a slightly smaller share of an ultimately much larger asset.

Whatever it is, I fear the Greeks even when they bring gifts.

Publius Vergilius Maro (Virgil)
ancient Roman Poet, 70 BC-19 BC

There are several wrong reasons to enter into a partnership, though. One of the deadliest is to grant somebody a stake in the company because he happens to bring a big customer or other source of business along with him. The pitfall here is that you actually buy nothing but a bit of turnover – if that. Once on board, the attached person can quickly turn into a foreign body within your company, running his own shop-in-a-shop beyond anyone else's control. Worse, he may develop into a possibly annoying collateral when the business he brought as a wedding gift disappoints or disappears. So whenever you consider inviting someone to a partnership, ask yourself the million dollar question. Would you be interested in partnering with the man or woman if there weren't any sweetener involved? Tread carefully. Always have two or three of your biggest supporters interview him or her, without informing them of what he or she has promised you to bring along.

I don't need a friend who changes when I change and who nods when I nod; my shadow does that much better.

PLUTARCH

You should also avoid partnering with people who are just like you. If you want to leverage who you are and what you're able to do yourself, it's better to do this with the help of like-minded, more junior people (if at all). On partner level, however, you can and should allow for a variety of personalities and skills. Partners should have the maturity and independency of mind to allow for dissent, which is necessary to avoid group think, to look beyond the status quo, to see troubles ahead and to spot new opportunities. If this variety of views is absent, battles based on overlapping competencies are sure to emerge all the same. Better, then, to accept that battles will take place anyhow, preferably with new ideas and well-founded policies as a result rather than just a momentary settling of who is granted the status of top dog.

Never have a companion that casts you in the shade.

BALTASAR GRACIÁN

Spanish Jesuit author, 1601-1658

If you look for complementary skills in your partners, you reduce the risk of peer pressure as it plagues any team which lacks such multi-discipline quality. Equally important, you should also verify whether a new partner is as fond of you and the rest of the partnership as he is of himself. You don't want Sun Kings who consider themselves the center of the universe; they consider you very, very fortunate at being exposed to their Midas touch. You can usually spot this type of person by their royal demeanor and by their constant, automatic claiming of your ideas and work as their own. This is often not done consciously, but rather as an animal reflex; some people just cannot stand the thought of somebody else conceiving or making anything valuable without them being involved. Being self-obsessed, they are always ready to bask in deserved and undeserved glory. Extreme cases of the type would almost accept your personal compliment to them for today's beautiful weather.

I think you can write very good comedy without a partner, but what I love about it, working with a partner, is that you get to places you'd never get to on your own. It's like when God was designing the world and decided we couldn't have children without a partner; it was a way of mixing up the genes so you'd get a more interesting product.

John Cleese

Considering all the possible difficulties and disappointments that come with partnerships, you might wonder whether you should entertain the thought of entering into one or more of them at all. The answer is: it depends. Do your homework and check the criteria as outlined in the introduction of this chapter. But allow yourself to be surprised as well. Great cooperation between equals can emerge spontaneously and without a pre-conceived plan. You'll know it when you find yourself engaged in it.

15 Firing people

Sacking employees is the second hardest job to do as an entrepreneur, especially when it is for reasons like cost cutting due to bad business for which these very employees are not directly accountable. Even harder, of course, is to keep people employed who are obviously not up to the task and won't ever be. Should you find yourself in this situation, you might want to do some hard thinking about what made you hire them in the first place, and who has been fooling who.

An 'unemployed' existence is a worse negation of life than death itself.

José Ortega y Gasset (attributed)
Spanish philosopher and essayist, 1883-1955

Irrespective of whether the man or woman you're firing was up to any good or not, you should never forget that being bounced out of a job can be one of the most dramatic events in a person's life. Admittedly, this awareness should in no way influence your decision to cut someone loose. It may, however, guide you as to the tonality you choose and the empathy you show when doing it. Likewise for the efforts you may want to undertake to help the employee find a new position elsewhere.

Strong managers who make tough decisions to cut jobs provide the only true job security in today's world. Weak managers are the problem. Weak managers destroy jobs.

JACK WELCH (ATTRIBUTED)

American business executive, 1935

One could indeed argue that any redundancy that should take place but doesn't, puts more jobs in danger. The opportunity cost can be considerable. Just remember that every precious payroll dollar can only be spent once. Make your employees worth every penny.

I saw the head chef at the Hotel Majestic fire a pastry cook because the poor devil could not get his brioches to rise straight. This ruthlessness made all the other chefs feel that they were working in the best kitchen in the world.

DAVID OGILVY

It's not only about wasting money, though. If you let non-performers underachieve without addressing the issue, your more professional crew will take this as an insult. At the very least, they will feel questioned as to their own capabilities.

The first essential for a Prime Minister is to be a good butcher.

WILLIAM GLADSTONE
British politician, 1809-1898

Once you have made up your mind to lay off people, you should act without delay. Especially in smaller organizations, it will be impossible to hide that the axe is about to fall. So if you can afford it, have the people whose employment you are terminating leave the company as quickly as possible, although this may mean doling out some severance payment and dealing with possible organizational hiccups. Bad employees whose contract is terminated and who hang around until the end of the notice period will spread gloom and therefore detract other workers. Good employees will be frustrated if they have to stay along when the dismissal is not their fault, but caused by force majeure. This will, again, rub off on other workers. So if you must let people go, do it as quickly as possible. And remember: nobody is irreplaceable, including you.

16 Managing trade relations

The importance of business relations can vary widely. Some are as valuable as your key employees, others are somewhat exchangeable. Let us focus on the connections where the stakes are high, although that said, managing a multitude of relations which are each of moderate importance is an art form in itself.

There is no friendship in trade.

CORNELIUS VANDERBILT
American businessman, 1794-1877

Trade relations have a utilitarian character and do not exist for their own sake, contrary to what can be the case with love and friendship. It must be added that the difference may not necessarily be large. After all, lovers and friends usually trade favors and benefits as well. And a longer-term, mutually profitable business-like exchange may well create friendship as a happy by-product.

It is not from the benevolence of the butcher, the brewer, or the baker, that we expect our dinner, but from their regard to their own self-interest. We address ourselves, not to their humanity but to their self-love, and never talk to them of our own necessities but of their advantages.

ADAM SMITH
Scottish moral philosopher, pioneer of political economy, 1723-1790

It is good that others make a decent amount of money off you. It means that they have a vested interest in adding value for you. This, in turn, ensures timely delivery of quality goods and services at a reasonable price and with good customer support, both now and in the future. One mature advertising agency client regularly asks his agency whether they are sure that they're still making a fair profit on his account. He knows that if this is no longer the case, his mandate sooner or later will be rated second priority. He realizes that he is competing continuously for the maximum share of a scarce resource: the time and attention from the agency's top talent.

It is your concern when your neighbor's wall is on fire.

QUINTUS HORATIUS FLACCUS (HORACE)
Ancient Roman poet, 65 BC-8 BC

Not only does a great deal of your well-being depend on

that of your trade partners, you are also exposed to the same risks which they run. Think of your raw material supplier encountering shortages, your distributor losing grip on his territory or your consultancy experiencing talent drain. Not your problem? You bet it is. If any of these troubles materialize, your own value chain will suffer almost immediately, irrespective of whether you can hold the supplier liable for the ensuing damages. So be sure that your suppliers are healthy. You can do your part by paying them fair prices and settling their bills on time.

It is only by not paying one's bills that one can hope to live in the memory of the commercial classes.

OSCAR WILDE

Irish essayist, novelist, playwright and poet, 1854-1900

You should not expect more from business acquaintances than is commensurate with their main function: helping you to make money. Your counterparts expect nothing more from you either. With economic motives being the main reason for both parties to engage with each other and with economic conditions changing all the time, you will quickly forget and be forgotten once this tangible benefit has evaporated for one or both parties. That's life. Be prepared to accept a lot of entering and erasing in your address book without hard feelings.

Be civil to all; sociable to many; familiar with few; friend to one; enemy to none.

BENJAMIN FRANKLIN

polymath, co-founder of the United States, 1706-1790

In short, be realistic about what you can and cannot expect from business contacts. Don't project personal longings for attachment and dialogue in whatever way into trade relations. It will cost you dearly. And it's not fair to the other party either. Again, when a non-business dimension emerges while working together, you should not necessarily shy away from it. Dealing with somebody in a business environment for some time can be a great way for other sympathies between people to emerge. Just don't set off with these expectations. Realize that when a connection evolves into something more personal, its original business use will inevitably suffer. Having said that, you should not be too selective or shy in your dealings with other people just because they cannot fulfill the role of life-long lover, friend or trusted counsellor. There is no extra cost involved in acting in a polite, courteous manner to everybody.

17 Strategic thinking – embracing ambiguity

Searching the holy grail of strategy usually involves a lot of ho-hum. People put on their most pretentious face when they talk strategy. Consulting firms charge stiff hourly rates for anything involving the S word. But it all comes down to answering a couple of fairly straightforward questions. What are we really good at? What situation are we in? What would we like to achieve? Which alternative ways of committing our money and our abilities do we have to get there? What's the best way forward for us? What are we going to do right now? Simple as these questions may be, they have one thing in common: there is no single right answer to any of them. And while the goals may seem straightforward, the ways to achieve them are anything but. That's the paradox of strategy.

The philosophy of this world may be founded on facts, but its business is run on spiritual impressions and atmospheres.

G.K. Chesterton

Life on this planet often appears random and chaotic. Worse, the things which promise maximum stability and security, such as money, status, military power, the law, knowledge, friendship, religion and love, are eternally fluid and cannot be captured by anyone – at least not for longer periods of time and certainly not forever. Yet these same things are what everybody is continually after. But there is no safety and there is no guaranteed way to succeed or even survive.

Business? It's quite simple. It's other people's money.

ALEXANDRE DUMAS, JR.
French novelist and playwright, 1824-1895

Markets only consist of buyers who do not settle for the here and now: you cannot sell anything to someone who is fully content. Every business caters to some kind of elementary dream; the dream to be free, the dream to belong, the dream to endure or the dream to escape. As spin-offs, there are the more particular dreams of robust health, of relief from hunger or danger, of happiness, comfort, sexual pleasure, power, prestige, wealth, security and so on. In short, all business strategy starts with this vital question: whose elementary dream do you help to fulfill and what is it? This may well be your own dream, of course. As we discussed earlier, many inventions and new ventures are sparked by the inventor's personal fears, dissatisfactions and wishes.

It is the nature of all greatness not to be exact.

EDMUND BURKE

By definition, dreams, visions, good ideas and strategic plans have a certain ambiguous quality. Firstly, they should be broad enough to inspire a broader set of people who can all identify with it in some way. This means there must be room for interpretation and recognition by different persons with different interests and mental dispositions. Secondly, they should also allow for evolution over time. So you cannot be too specific, lest the whole thing appeals to only a few people, becomes outdated very quickly or both. Put differently, when we are talking strategy or for that matter, entrepreneurship as such, we are talking art rather than science.

You can use all the quantitative data you can get, but you still have to distrust it and use your own intelligence and judgment.

ALVIN TOFFLER

American writer and futurist, 1928

Keeping up this healthy ambiguity is not an easy task in the present Machine Age, where all people and all things must be classified and quantified. With today's daily stream of data about everybody and everything, it is tempting to lose track of qualitative, fairly timeless factors such as the buyer's core motives which entice him to part with his money and which are the reason of existence for your company. But there are plenty of other dangers that come with information overload as well. As statisticians know, big data can lead to plenty of useless facts. Think of chance correlations between events that look fascinating but actually tell you nothing, because there is no causality between them. Then there is the terror of continuously new, changing, futile information. Take the daily glut of data on the financial markets. As any intelligent investor knows, hourly or daily fluctuations on the stock exchange are utterly meaningless. They do nothing but whip you up to frenetic trading activity which only costs you money.

Fate laughs at probabilities.

Edward Bulwer-Lytton

English novelist, playwright, and politician, 1803-1873

If that weren't enough, even deep computing still cannot predict any significant event, whether it's the oil price level six months from now, the next possible nuclear war, or the question if and when your sister will get married. As historians can tell you, many landmark historic events unfold in an unexpected way and at a largely unexpected time and place. As scientists can tell you, many great discoveries are made by accident, stumbled upon while they were busily looking for something else.

All in all, you should be very reluctant to rely on figures and statistics when occupying yourself with strategic choices. Statistics are only telling if they produce graphics that you only need to glance at once to see what's going on.

Life is so largely controlled by chance that its conduct can be but a perpetual improvisation.

W. Somerset Maugham

So much for Five Year Plans. At its core, developing and executing a good strategy means nothing but acutely observing what is going on, adapting your resources to the present situation and staying tuned. This is in order not to miss out on any major change out there that requires a commensurate change of direction.

18 Strategic thinking – preserving an independent mind

When putting together your strategic plan, not only should you allow for a good deal of ambiguity, you should also have the courage to fly alone. Specifically, you should avoid autopilot thinking and resist fashionable idées recues. Keep the perspective of a bird of prey: high up in the sky for a detached but clear overview, but ready to dive whenever the occasion requires it.

We are too much accustomed to attribute to a single cause that which is the product of several, and the majority of our controversies come from this.

Marcus Aurelius

ancient stoic philosopher and Roman emperor, 121-180

The tendency to simplify is pervasive in every neat business school case study and certainly in every success story. This is because a result-oriented, profit-oriented way of thinking as it prevails in business prefers quick, mediocre answers (often dressed up as great stories) to brilliant, difficult questions. But simple explanations are usually incomplete or even dead wrong. And if causes of a situation are more diverse than we think, it is also likely that most problems we want to tackle are more complex than we acknowledge. So resist the human tendency to cut corners.

I suppose it is tempting, if the only tool you have is a hammer, to treat everything as if it were a nail.

Abraham Maslow

American psychologist, 1908-1970

Defining problems really well is indeed a major success factor for entrepreneurs. It is the result of independent thinking, relentless curiosity and the willingness to put in long hours studying a problem. One could even argue that originality in problem definition is what makes entrepreneurs and their results stand out. The reason for this is that well-defined problems usually set you on track to find the right solutions. So the time you put in problem analysis is well-invested and leverages the effectiveness of what you subsequently conceive as a plan and what you are going to do. Master your impatience and look before you leap.

Before each new venture he studied the field for a long time, then proceeded to act as if he had never heard of it, upsetting all precedent.

Ayn Rand
Russian-American novelist, philosopher, playwright and screenwriter, 1905-1982

Indeed, simplification is most dangerous in the early stages of strategy development. Your action plan can never be more effective than your analysis, only less so. It is better to get to work with more or less reasonable solutions to complex problems which you have assessed thoroughly, than to have a perfect but totally irrelevant plan for an ill-defined problem. In short, reflect carefully, know when you've finished thinking, then act swiftly. Be like the smart buzzard. It uses the thermal currents to stay up in the air for long stretches of time without exhausting itself. It scans the territory until prey shows up and the opportunity arises to strike effectively.

It can scarcely be denied that the supreme goal of all theory is to make the irreducible basic elements as simple and as few as possible, without having to surrender the adequate representation of a single datum of experience. (often paraphrased as: Everything should be made as simple as possible, but not simpler.)

ALBERT EINSTEIN
German theoretical physicist, 1879-1955

Some business school professors or management gurus compare the development and deployment of a strategy to playing chess. Obviously, they have never been in business for one day in their entire lives. Compared to the well-structured army of chess pieces, your company's resources are a disorganized bunch. Instead of a neat set of 64 squares, your real-life playing field is more of a jungle. Instead of one single opponent to battle, you may have several. And they don't have exactly the same artillery as you. Moreover, fighting an adversary is not your prime objective in the first place. So in all its apparent sophistication, the chess game allegory is overly simplified and off the mark. The same goes for other analogies such as sports games and other forms of easy, domesticated, risk-free adventure. Using these comparisons equals an attempt to create order where there actually isn't any. For entrepreneurship, muddling through during the never ending political conflicts in the Middle East would be a better metaphor. There, as in real business life, goals are evolving, the availability of resources is subject to constant change, the competitive forces are shifting all the time, the allies are hard to count on and knowing when to accept one's losses and to settle or quit isn't easy.

Learn to see in another's calamity the ills which you should avoid.

PUBLILIUS SYRUS

Syrian-born writer of maxims, brought to Italy as a slave, fl. 85-43 BC

When strategizing, part of your observational powers should be geared to detecting key failure factors relevant to your business. You may infer them from other people's earlier unsuccessful activities. This is a low-cost way (at least for you) to steer clear of some cliffs, which may well save you a lot of time and money further down the road. No need here to feel an exploiter. The earlier sacrifices made and losses incurred by your unfortunate peers are sunk costs anyway. One caveat: avoid the same kind of simplifications mentioned above. The reasons for other people's failures may be manifold. Do you really know what happened? Moreover, not all of the factors may apply to your own situation. It may be that the scene has changed and that the others were just too early, a quite common reason for failed introductions of innovative products and services in particular.

Fortune is like the market, where many times, if you can stay a little, the price will fall.

Francis Bacon

English philosopher, politician and essayist, 1561-1626

Astutely, independently and patiently observing the outside world may not only teach you a thing or two about success and failure. It may also provide you with information needed for some good-old contrarian thinking such as seeing opportunities where nobody else does and practicing caution when everyone else is euphoric. Going against the grain and biding your time is in itself no guarantee for success. But it comes with some considerable advantages. You will avoid being drawn into the crowd and being harmed by its often erratic herd behavior. You will, for instance, avoid buying high and selling low, a costly habit which most people fall victim to.

The superior man understands what is right; the inferior man understands what will sell.

Confucius

Of course, an entrepreneur must meet both specifications expressed in this maxim, at least if he wants to make a profit. He cannot discard the second, commercially focused element as something beneath his dignity.

For him, the prime relevance of the saying lies in the right order of priorities that can be derived from it: put your own competence and your own convictions first. Use them to build the best product or service you can. Only when you're set in this respect should you start thinking of how to bring your value proposition to the market.

Another relevant interpretation of this same Confucian principle: avoid taking advantage of your customers, even if you would seem to get away with it. Don't sell them inferior stuff at inflated prices. Settle for making a little less money by offering them something which is their money's worth. The mental ease or even pride you will gain from this way of working will be invaluable. Your long-term market share may flourish as well.

19 Turning your strategy into action

When it comes to acting the part, there is one word which is of the utmost importance: time. Time is a decisive factor in many respects. Do you have enough of it, which is probably more than you think you'll need? And if there's time, do you have both the serenity and the discipline to spend enough of it? Do you have a sense of urgency? In other words, are you able to separate the chances and necessities here and now from the past and the future ones? Are you able to stage your activities accordingly?

The success of most things depends upon knowing how long it will take to succeed.

Charles-Louis de Secondat, Baron de La Brède et de Montesquieu (Montesquieu)

French lawyer, thinker and political philosopher, 1689-1755

Because of the human tendency to underestimate complexity, in business and elsewhere, things tend to take more time than expected. You are more dependent on third parties than you think. These parties have more on their mind than you realize and probably have priorities other than just pursuing your interests. And then there are those rare events which are impossible to predict but can have a severe impact on the time path of your plan. As a rule of thumb, even if you think you're pretty realistic, be sure to plan and calculate with a cautious, slightly pessimistic view. Write the key figures down. Done? Then double the total amounts of required time, money and other resources you have just defined.

Patience is the support of weakness; impatience the ruin of strength.

Charles Caleb Colton

English clergyman, writer and art collector, 1780-1832

There is this strange phenomenon of the same person, idea or product being rejected at one time and place and then being cordially welcomed at another. That's the way the world turns and it is not easy to accept if you are convinced of the soundness of your enterprise and its proposition, full of drive to conquer the world and anxious to stop the cash draining away instead of coming in. It can be hard to stay serene when results take more time to materialize than you think would be necessary. You are especially prone to this type of impatience if you possess a high level of energy and a good deal of intellect. If that's the case, your mind is sure to travel faster than reality can keep up with. When encountering delays, you may try to overdo it and force your way through, stepping up efforts and investments. And probably to no avail. Avoid your mental assets turning into liabilities and keep your cool.

Expansion means complexity and complexity decay.

C. Northcote Parkinson

English historian and author, 1909-1993

Building a mega jet which carries eight hundred passengers is not like building one small, single engine plane eight hundred times over. It won't be 'more of the same' in many respects. You will have to deal with all kinds of new challenges. They could include new and more complex aerodynamics, larger and more sophisticated research and manufacturing facilities, new and more intricate financing, more detailed and much longer production processes. Plus a totally different marketing landscape, with plenty of parties involved, in a tedious decision making process.

Ditto for geographical expansion. Having three hundred car dealerships across the continent does not equal operating three local ones and then multiplied by one hundred. Again, you will meet all kinds of new challenges such as varying market conditions per country, differences in legislation and totally new supply chain matters. Geographic expansion will also force you to make yourself accustomed to cultures to which you may find adaptation problematic.

No matter what shape your expansion comes in, you

will probably need to hire many more people. You will no longer be able to recruit and manage them alone. Also your increased need for capital will lead to the involvement of new financial parties who will have their own set ways vis-á-vis governance. In short, all expansion comes with more control by others and less by you.

The massive reduction in risk that is inherent in the development of the modern corporation has been far from fully appreciated.

JOHN KENNETH GALBRAITH
Canadian-American economist and author, 1908-2006

So play it safe and settle for small? Hold it right there. Certainly, there are specific risks attached to that as well. Your home-sweet-home market within easy driving distance may suddenly be plagued by local unemployment and by associated fall in demand. Or local business is booming and office rents spiral out of control. If you are in an increasingly certified industry, the costs for accreditation may become prohibitive for small players. Stepped up legal compliance demands may also become a headache. Concentration of your industry may lead to bigger competitors with lower costs and more investment power. And if your scale of operations becomes ever more limited relative to competition, you may not be able to attract and pay top talent anymore. Small, as a consequence, is not always beautiful or even feasible.

Furthermore, your loss of control due to scaling up is only relative. After all, you will now command a bigger resource base and work a bigger market. It's just that it won't be as much of a one-man show as you are accustomed to. So when opportunities for expansion present themselves, just be certain that you are willing to give up the fine art of micromanagement. Not being able to do so is one of the key reasons why businesses stay smaller than they could have been.

No lesson seems to be so deeply inculcated by the experience of life as that you should never trust experts. If you believe doctors, nothing is wholesome: if you believe the theologians, nothing is innocent: if you believe the soldiers, nothing is safe. They all require their strong wine diluted by a very large admixture of insipid common sense.

Robert Gascoyne-Cecil, 3rd Marquess of Salisbury

British politician, 1830-1903

The mixed blessing of experts is that they have the potential to put you both on and off the right track. Experts know more about important subjects than you do (say the law, or IT, or accounting), so they may protect you against yourself and may help you make balanced decisions. But experts often have a hard time accepting that they do not amount to much in a given situation. They tend to exaggerate the importance of their profession, led by either consciousness or vanity. Their worst fear is to have overlooked risks involved with a certain situation, so they will tend to be pessimistic and to exaggerate problems.

Manage your experts well. Be sure that they have too much work so that they are forced to set priorities as to what to bother about. Ensure frequent interaction with other departments in order for their ideas to remain practical. Also, create enough unscheduled time and quiet surroundings for them to be able to retreat. Listen carefully to them, show interest in their expertise and ask them to explain their views in language which you can understand. This should not impose any difficulties. Real experts are able to rise above details without oversimplifying.

If you see ten troubles coming down the road, you can be sure that nine will run into the ditch before they reach you and you have to battle with only one of them.

CALVIN COOLIDGE

American president, 1872-1933

Paranoia is nothing but a state of excessive consciousness. You sense all possible dangers, including the ones which do not materialize and probably never will. Just remember: if all conceivable trouble actually happened to all of us, our species would have gone under long ago. Yes, a big client of yours may terminate his contract. Yes, your best salesman may quit. Yes, you may be drawn into an unforeseeable product liability lawsuit. But unless your planetary constellations are extreme, not all of this will happen to you and certainly not all at the same time.

Never let the future disturb you. You will meet it, if you have to, with the same weapons of reason which today arm you against the present.

Marcus Aurelius

The trouble that does not actually run into the ditch will be easiest to meet head-on once it presents itself. Rest assured that you are a much better improviser than you think. Big scenario planning for each conceivable event is both useless and impossible. Likewise for all kinds of time-consuming and money-draining provisions and precautions. Exceptions are things like sound security procedures at a production site and insurances for small-probability events with extreme consequences.

It was the same with the whole Russian machine. Fear was the impulse. For them it was always safer to advance than retreat. Advance against the enemy and the bullet might miss you. Retreat, evade, betray and the bullet would never miss.

IAN FLEMING

English author, journalist and naval intelligence officer, 1908-1964

Once you're on track, no matter with how much enthusiasm you have kicked off, withdrawal should always be an option. Avoid soldiering on for its own sake when the situation makes this no longer feasible. You may still succeed, but the sacrifices may be out of any proportion. Don't fall victim to the so-called sunk cost fallacy, also known as 'throwing good money after bad'. This good money is lost forever for more promising alternatives. The best way to avoid this mental lock is to have an exit plan B available right from the start. And to build a continuously updated idea bank with attractive other opportunities to switch to.

20 Getting advice

Just like your in-house experts, external consultants can both add and destroy value at your enterprise. Judging them is a tricky task, as you cannot fully assess their expertise and thus their diligence on the job or, ultimately, whether they are worth the money. "I don't know your craft, but I can smell who's good at it," is the way one entrepreneur once summarized his reliance on gut feeling when he hired an attorney. As always when buying services, making some calls for references is another risk-reducing exercise.

No enemy is worse than bad advice.

SOPHOCLES

ancient Greek playwright, dramatist, priest and politician, 496 BC-406 BC

The problem with bad advice is that it is often followed for too long. After all, advice is solicited based on uncertainty and doubt (absent this state of mind there is no need to search for it in the first place). In other words when your position is vulnerable. So trust is an important factor. Trust, however, means giving the advisor and his plans the benefit of the doubt, which in turn means delay. Delay in recognizing that the approach might not work, delay in doing something about it and delay in discharging the advisor. During this delay, the opportunity costs may be mounting, together with the advisor's accumulating time expenditure and fees. The consultant's stiff monthly bills can actually add to the delay. It takes courage to admit that the money paid to date has not bought you useful results yet and, worse, probably won't buy you either from now on. It's the sunk cost fallacy in full swing.

All professions are conspiracies against the laity.

GEORGE BERNARD SHAW

The challenges you encounter when you mobilize in-house experts as dealt with in the previous chapter, are the same ones you meet when chartering external advisors, only more so. Let's face it, whoever works at a daily or hourly rate, without long term job security and on an income which is highly based on actually billable hours, will tend to inflate the importance of his trade even more than an in-house expert on a steady payroll contract. It would be superhuman not to. So in consulting, there is never a strict division between advising and selling. By definition the interests are aligned to only a limited extent. When was the last time that you heard an asset manager suggest that you stay out of securities altogether? Or an ad executive proposing that you reduce the marketing-communications budget to zero?

Or a corporate finance advisor recommending that you should not engage in merging or selling your business? There is no such thing as fully impartial advice.

If you want work well done, select a busy man, the other kind has no time.

Elbert Hubbard

American writer, artist and philosopher, 1856-1915

To minimize this conflict of interest, look for advisors who are fully employed and aren't desperate for your business. They will not make mountains out of molehills to keep themselves financially afloat. Also, look for advisors who have low overheads. If they run a tight ship themselves, they will do the same on your behalf. One further way to select your advisors is to weed out the most pretentious fellows. Lawyers who label themselves 'boardroom counsellor'. Accountants who claim the Most Trusted Advisor badge of honor. PR agency men who have revamped themselves into some kind of visionary guru – you get the picture. These types are the first you should quickly delete from your shortlist. Finally, avoid advisors who present themselves as genuine partners in business. They are not. They do not share your risks.

There are some men who turn a deaf ear to reason and good advice and wilfully go wrong for fear of being controlled.

Jean de La Bruyère

French essayist and moralist, 1645-1696

Let's not be too hard on the consulting profession, though. There are plenty of decent, hard-working experts around who have the honest goal of helping you and your business to get results and at reasonable prices. Chances are that they have stronger skills than you and your in-house staff, at least in their field of specialization. Are you mature enough to acknowledge this, and to give them the floor? And how about your specialized staff? You should realize that the best freelancers are better than the average or even the best experts on the payroll. They may outdo your department in non-conformist creative thinking or in highly domain-specific expertise. Avoid using them for more process-oriented tasks without a clear beginning or end. They are too expensive for that and interfering with going concern will create bad blood with your regular staff as well.

I owe my success to having listened respectfully to the very best advice, and then going away and doing the exact opposite.

G.K. Chesterton

The problem with advice is that it costs a lot of money. Money which the average businessman hates to spend unless there are clear-cut, short-term benefits to be derived from it. So in an ideal yet non-existent world, the advice should have generated additional profit well before the payment of the consultants' bill. The consultants know this, of course and will be wary of advising anything with an ambiguous character or with a predominantly long-term effect. If they have the natural urge to do so nevertheless, they will probably resort to other modalities than consulting, such as writing a book (sic). Sticking to consulting, they will tend to advise the client according to what he already expects, lest he refuses to accept their invoices. They will circle around the status quo: maybe one step ahead, but no more. Again, there is often no marked difference between consulting and selling. Unless of course you create that rare climate in which your advisors can speak their mind without fear of being rejected and without jeopardizing their income.

In the end, it's all up to you. It takes a good client for a consultant to produce valuable advice. If you, as a customer, can avoid the path of least resistance, so can your consultants. If you can't, there is no point in hiring them in the first place.

21 Building a company culture

There are many definitions of the topic but let's keep it simple. Company culture is how you would like your staff to act without you being around and without hard rules and sanctions to enforce it. In this respect, the shape of your company culture is an indicator of your leadership qualities covered in earlier chapters.

The greatest way to live with honor in this world is to be what we pretend to be.

SOCRATES (ATTRIBUTED)

Ironically, the most valued principles in life hardly need any reinforcement. Or they shouldn't. How comfortable would you feel if your lover told you three times a day how much he or she cared for you? You'd doubtless prefer to have these statements translated into a steady flow of sensitive gestures, great and small. No doubt you would rather talk the talk and walk the walk yourself as well. With company culture it's very much the same. The principles you would probably like to see acted upon (say integrity, hard work, a cooperative spirit, a quest for quality) are so universal that they should be put into practice without the need of dedicated advertisement. To proclaim them constantly all over the place ('Our

Number One Priority Is The Customer') will reap disdain, boredom and alienation.

The best executive is the one who has sense enough to pick good men to do what he wants done, and self-restraint enough to keep from meddling with them while they do it.

THEODORE ROOSEVELT
American president, 1858-1919

The dangers of micromanagement mentioned earlier are especially valid in case of dealing with culture. Having a list of dos and don'ts available for every day interaction between people is not only patronizing, but such manuals will look more incomplete and inept the more extensive they become. A Code of Conduct with umpteen pages will be skimmed at best by its target audience, then quickly forgotten. Instead of creating new bibles, focus on the essentials. What is the number one goal everybody at your organization must work to? Think about the sports car maker Lamborghini, whose original overriding target was to build a faster car than Ferrari, full stop. What is *your* main objective? Also, be clear about your priorities. Who are your number one stakeholders? The shareholders? The staff? The customers? They cannot be equally important. In all truth, what relative weight would you grant each of them? What does the company ask from them? What does it give back? In short: what's the deal? How about your view on possible conflicts of interest? Try to make difficult but enlightening choices here. They will stick in the mind much better than hopeless clichés like 'people being our most important asset' and so forth.

My people and I have come to an agreement which satisfies us both. They are to say what they please, and I am to do what I please.

FREDERICK THE GREAT (ATTRIBUTED)
King of Prussia, 1712-1786

Having a sound company culture full of active participation by every individual is a wonderful thing but there are of course limits to self-regulation. Even in an enlightened corporate climate, resources are still limited and alignments of interest between individuals, departments or stakeholder groups are never perfect. A good company culture does not take away the burden on your part to make decisions, including tough ones. Rather, it ensures that the decisions you have to make are of a better quality. There will, for instance, be less need to waste time on settling counterproductive internal battles.

In a time of drastic change it is the learners who inherit the future. The learned usually find themselves equipped to live in a world that no longer exists.

ERIC HOFFER

American moral and social philosopher, 1898-1983

Allow for a significant allotment of time and money for training for everybody at your organization. Every employee should be granted, say, one or two weeks off for studying annually and a tuition fee budget equal to one or two weeks' pay. This investment, equal to about five percent of your total headcount costs, will pay for itself handsomely. Newcomers and old hands alike will value that the company invests in them. They will get back from their program refreshed and no doubt with a good idea or two.

Knowledge is of two kinds. We know a subject ourselves, or we know where we can find information upon it.

SAMUEL JOHNSON

Leverage everybody's minds and skills continuously by sharing new insights, gained through educational timeouts or otherwise. Have regular informal lunches and drinks with small groups to exchange knowledge and ideas By the way, when was the last time you had two weeks off for some solid new learning yourself?

22 Negotiation

A large part of business life consists of bartering with other people in order to get what you want. When you are about to enter such a situation, the first thing you should do is avoid popular preconceptions of successful negotiators as created by Hollywood screenwriters. You know, tough guys in military uniforms or sharp bespoke suits, who relentlessly push their opponent into a tiny corner and then grab everything that's on the table, girl included. Real life is not like that. The best negotiators aim for maximum mutual benefit.

Power concedes nothing without a demand. It never did and it never will.

FREDERICK DOUGLASS

American social reformer, abolitionist, orator, writer and politician, former slave, c. 1818-1895

That said, it may be a rough ride before parties are ready to settle. Much depends on the extent to which interests can be aligned. Power games develop when conflicts of interest dominate the scene and overshadow possible complementarity or mutuality. Good negotiators succeed in redefining the former into the latter as much as possible, though probably not in full.

You only have power over people so long as you don't take everything away from them. But when you've robbed a man of everything, he's no longer in your power – he's free again.

ALEKSANDR SOLZHENITSYN

Russian novelist, dramatist and historian,1918-2008

The good news is that you're not the only one who needs others to get something. Every time you find yourself invited to a bargaining event, you should realize that you wouldn't meet at all if the other party saw no benefit attached to you. Build on that knowledge. Try to put yourself in your counterpart's shoes. What is his agenda? What does he want? What does he need without possibly realizing it yet? The better your insight into these matters, the more value you can bring to the table and the stronger your bargaining position will be.

Necessity never made a good bargain.

BENJAMIN FRANKLIN

Though you should not use this option lightheartedly, it is good to remember that you can always walk away from any negotiation. You can then choose from different alternative options such as doing nothing at all or deploying other actions, such as taking the thing to court, mobilizing other parties for extra bargaining power or developing other independent activity. Being aware of this exit option will help you avoid feeling trapped and accepting unfavorable settlements. It's like the difference between successful and less successful managers. Research suggests that the latter tend to feel unduly dependent on their present employer.

Some people have a knack of putting upon you gifts of no real value, to engage you to substantial gratitude. We thank them for nothing.

Charles Lamb
English essayist and poet, 1775-1834

Negotiation is an art. It has no scientific basis and it lacks a concise book of rules. Defining the central issue at stake is even more important but also even harder than it is in a courtroom. As a result, a good deal of rhetoric is always involved in the process. To drive home points of view, rational arguments and critical reasoning are mixed with tricks such as clever storytelling, humor, playing on the other party's emotions and other more or less manipulative techniques. Skilled players are able to make you feel obliged with a minimum of factual reasons. Con artists take this even further. To recognize them is to be able to handle them.

If he who employs coercion against me could mould me to his purposes by argument, no doubt he would. He pretends to punish me because his argument is strong; but he really punishes me because his argument is weak.

William Godwin

English journalist, political philosopher and novelist, 1756-1836

If your opponent tries to instill an unnecessary sense of obligation or fear in your mind or overdoes it on rhetoric in any other way, this is a sign of weakness. Instead of being intimidated by it you should be mildly amused. You actually have the upper hand! This insight enables you to take the lead in what should evolve as a fact-based discussion geared to mutual benefits.

Never allow a person to tell you no who doesn't have the power to say yes.

Eleanor Roosevelt (attributed)

American social activist and first lady, 1884-1962

As an entrepreneur, you are indeed likely to meet people at the table who are from organizations which are far more bureaucratic than your own company. Consequently, you always run the risk of dealing with representatives who actually have no authorization themselves. This can make for a frustrating process. You think you almost have a deal, only to find out that the other person needs to get back to his boss. You can guess the rest. A few days later he reports back to you that the boss, sadly and really, really quite unexpectedly, cannot agree to the terms which the two of you have hammered out.

There is no dead sure way to avoid this turn of events. You should find out the decision making unit and process as early as possible. You should also not give away anything in early discussions, and not too much along the way. Alternatively, you could demand that you speak to the final decisionmakers. Ensure that there is an equal level of authority talking on both sides of the table at all times.

The charms of the woman passing by are usually in direct ratio to the swiftness of her passing.

MARCEL PROUST

French novelist, essayist and critic, 1871-1922

Quick decisions tend to be decisions where you pay too much. Everything looks more attractive from afar. Only when taking a closer look, you spot the imperfections and possibly the serious flaws. Be sure to think through all aspects of a deal. Take your time, also and especially when the other party tries to rush you into a decision.

Delay is the deadliest form of denial.

C. Northcote Parkinson

Dealing with delay is like dealing with jealousy between lovers: a bit of it may increase the commitment, but too much of it will cause the relationship to blow up. In general, you should avoid playing the waiting game: it may lead to annoyance on the other guy's part, to a loss of trust and therefore to a lower chance of a mutually beneficial solution being accomplished. Just remember that without proper cultivation, every initiative dies a little every day. If there are good reasons why you must postpone decisions, be as specific and forthwith as possible about them to the other party. This will automatically ensure that you are honest to yourself as well. Do you want a deal to be closed or not?

23 Networking

As we have seen in previous chapters, running a business involves continuous interaction with other people. Your network is the total of persons with whom you have a somewhat meaningful contact. Research by social scientists such as Dunbar suggests that the number of these meaningful contacts which any individual can maintain at any time is around 150. This questions the value of the 500+ connections as claimed today by many persons on their online social network pages. Indeed, as many of these super-networkers will admit in private, most of these contacts cannot and do not amount to much. But nowadays everybody seems to have thousands of connections, so nobody wants to stay behind. While this bidding game is relatively harmless in private life (though probably causing some disappointments there as well), it can lead to a dangerous waste of precious time and effort for entrepreneurs.

Alone, adj. In bad company.

AMBROSE BIERCE

American journalist, writer and satirist, 1842-c. 1914

Since your capacity for keeping contacts is limited in the

first place, you should pursue a quality-based strategy. Don't engage in networking for reasons akin to herd behavior. By all means go out, but choose your venues carefully. Specifically, avoid networking events which are heavily branded as such. The scene will be dominated by people who are on a dedicated, narrowly-focused selling mission which is probably of no interest to you. Also, limit the time you spend on networking as a whole, be it at social events or on internet hubs. Each week, allow yourself a maximum of one or two dedicated real-life events and four or five one-hour sessions on virtual platforms. When you attend a real-life event, never dole out business cards indiscriminately. Also, avoid being the first one to enter and the last one to leave. A good, professional networker is not a party animal.

Go to parties!

Nassim Nicholas Taleb

In spite of this necessary caution, networking is a great way nevertheless to encounter people, especially people with ideas, skills, connections and other resources which are different from yours. So allow yourself the chance to be pleasantly surprised and to create unforeseen chemistry and new opportunities. Leave your comfort zone. Go to unfamiliar, one-off events on a regular basis. When choosing which venues to attend, the trick is indeed to resist the usual. Avoid meeting the same predictable people over and over again. Your weekly service club lunch with the usual complacent suspects at the table will do your business no good. And unless you happen to be a private banker with huge acquisition targets (and maybe also if you are), avoid hanging around on that good old golf course or at that same football pitch every weekend.

Knowing how to keep a friend is more important than gaining a new one.

Baltasar Gracián

Something to keep in mind when going out. Given the limited human capacity to maintain relationships, each new network contact is at the expense of existing ones. This is not a bad thing or a good thing in itself, it's just something to remember. Compare the situation to your compact bookshelf which contains, say, 150 beloved books which you like to take out and browse over on a regular basis. Any newly acquired work means an item of your present collection has to go. Always ask yourself, is that new acquisition worth discarding one of my trusted companions? Have I neglected some of them lately, for no good reason? Are there even some among them which I have not read and discovered to the end? Whenever a new acquaintance is in the making, hold still for a moment and scan your existing network too.

If a man does not make new acquaintance as he advances through life, he will soon find himself left alone. A man, Sir, should keep his friendship in constant repair.

SAMUEL JOHNSON

Maybe the gradual shift in your library and, by the same token, in your social network is only healthy. As we discussed before, life changes, you change yourself and so does your business. Go over your shelves regularly. Some books you will want to keep; some are ready to be exchanged for others. You are done reading them, have absorbed what they have to offer you and are ready to put them back into circulation. This should be done respectfully, of course. Maybe you want to honor your former acquaintances by recommending them to somebody else. On with them, to a new reader who will benefit more from them than you will.

Be very circumspect in the choice of your company. In the society of your equals you shall enjoy more pleasure; in the society of your superiors you shall find more profit. To be the best of the company is the way to grow worse; the best means to grow better is to be the worst there.

FRANCIS QUARLES
English poet, 1592-1644

When engaging yourself in networking on behalf of

your business, you should look for something more productive than just having a good time with people whom you feel comfortable with. Raise the bar a little and venture into networks which consist of people who are, in one way or another, a bit ahead of you. Not too much, by the way, or there will be no fruitful exchange. Compare this to playing tennis. You advance your game quickest by playing with people who are slightly better players than you are.

Be cautious in your intercourse with the great, they seldom confer obligations on their inferiors but from interested motives. Friendly they appear as long as it serves their turn, but they will render no assistance in time of actual need.

TALMUD

It is tempting to get in touch with people who are in a totally different league from yours in terms of wealth, power or abilities, and who in theory could leverage your business. But you should be reluctant to approach them. And when you do get to meet them, don't overestimate the use of the connection. The high and mighty are accustomed to keeping a safe distance from the rest of the world. They delegate many of their decisions to their generals, or rely on expensive advisors. So if at all possible, use references and be prepared to use two or three intermediary steps to get to any big shot. Once you encounter one in person, don't get carried away. His courtesy to you as such does not mean a lot; he probably deals this way with everybody. Of course, when you are convinced that you really have something special and valuable to offer him, go ahead and state your business.

Not to attend at the door of the wealthy, and not to use the voice of petition – these constitute the best life of a man.

HITOPADESA

In your dealings with the rich and famous, you should be polite and attentive but by no means servile. Don't tell them how wonderful you think they are. Usually, they are already surrounded by plenty of people who do that. Instead, get to the point quickly and make your well-prepared pitch as short and sweet as possible. Ensure that you are on a friendly basis with their assistants and other direct reports if you want any useful follow-up to materialize.

In the United States, doing good has come to be, like patriotism, a favorite device of persons with something to sell.

H. L. MENCKEN

Many people think that involving themselves with charity circles is the road to influence and power. Indeed, you will hardly find anybody (in the US or elsewhere) who actively engages in philanthropy without some kind of hidden agenda which has nothing to do with noble causes. Think of that machine gun manufacturer who wants to buy respectability by opening a fine art museum for his fellow men. Or think of that anonymous securities trader, who realizes his accumulated chance wealth will not buy him the longed-for peace of mind, much less immortal glory, and who decides to throw some feel-good crumbs to some disadvantaged youngsters.

Absent hard performance criteria, at practicing charity everyone's a winner. As a result, the sector not only attracts some bright, diligent and well-meaning professionals, but also a good deal of second rate talent: people who have not been able to really make it in business and who yearn for a certificate of nobility, without a serious personal downside or even the slightest accountability attached to it (who, in other words, like to obtain something for nothing). In addition, you will meet many people who in spite of a thin humanitarian veneer actually have a hard commercial interest rather than anything else (think of asset managers who double as charity trust board members). Unless you have the stomach to deal with this type of individuals, avoid the philanthropic networks altogether. If you want to do good, do it without anybody noticing it. Okay, maybe tell your wife and children and one or two friends.

I prefer the company of peasants because they have not been educated sufficiently to reason incorrectly.

Michel de Montaigne

Instead, your network should include plenty of people who are down to earth, free from the urge to be somebody and without vested interests worth mentioning. Not only are they fun to be with but they also speak their uncompromised – and often surprisingly witty – mind and help you to keep your own feet firmly on the ground. Try to be a bit like them yourself, and networking might actually turn into fun.

It is the final test of a gentleman – his respect for those who can be of no possible service to him.

William Lyon Phelps

American author, critic and scholar, 1865-1943

Once your business is well-developed and you have

reached a certain level of power, influence and success yourself, people with whom you are connected will in turn reach out to you for various forms of support. Be sure that your memory serves you well: treat them the way you would have liked to be treated yourself while you were on your way up. If there is little or no potential, at least be gracious about it. If you like what they're up to, lend a hand and arrange one or two introductions on their behalf.

24 Competition

To be commercially active means that you are most likely competing with others for your customer's money. Even if you're the only pizza parlor in town, you are still competing with the tapas bar down the road, or with the alternative plain and simple home cooking option. Realizing this should help you to stay tuned and to constantly offer value at fair prices, thus ensuring your company's long-term viability.

Competition enlivens business.

German saying

When the supply side consists of a number of different, competitive parties, who all offer good quality as well, this may add to the over-all visibility and attractiveness of the product category you're in. This, in turn, may increase the sales volume of the total market and may well benefit every individual supplier, including you. Think of all those high-end fashion boutiques which have flocked together in the same uptown area. Collectively they offer a more attractive shopping environment than if they were the only one in the neighborhood. Or, when it's about attracting staff rather than customers, consider the advantage of being located in a geographic area where all major industry players are concentrated, and which can therefore turn into a true talent magnet, such as Silicon Valley.

He that wrestles with us strengthens our nerves, and sharpens our skill. Our antagonist is our helper.

Edmund Burke

To have competitors means that you have assets and objectives which others consider worth wile. In business you should rate competition a confirmation that you are on the right track. Competitors may even enlighten you about your strengths and your opportunities. Learn as much as possible from them, without every step you take being influenced by them.

Whenever men are not obliged to fight from necessity, they fight from ambition; which is so powerful in human breasts, that it never leaves them no matter to what rank they rise.

Niccolò Machiavelli

Don't let yourself be pulled into some kind of battle just for the thrill of beating others at your game. Everybody can buy short-term, unprofitable, unsustainable market share. Be aware that every growth, certainly if bought at low margins, involves new risks. Some pitches you should be happy not to win.

Divide and rule.

Julius Caesar (attributed)

ancient Roman military and political leader, 100 BC - 44 BC

These days there is a lot of media uproar about companies which violate the rules of fair competition. While there is certainly a lot of misconduct around in this respect, the demand side's power play is partially responsible for this climate as well. Especially in the business-to-business market, large corporations and governmental bodies nowadays tend to organize massive tenders. They request umpteen potential suppliers to come up with thick, detailed proposals for even moderately-sized orders. In service industries in particular, the capitalized time expenditure which these purchasing procedures require may eat up a good deal of a company's profit.

This is not to say that you should bend the rules in order to optimize your chance of winning business. Rather, you should try to develop a sixth sense for timewasters who possibly even without senior management's authorization invite half the globe to draw up proposals. Beware and never do any significant work just to get on some kind of longlist. Even if you are told that you have passed some initial selection process already, you should always find out how many candidates are being invited to tender and what the selection criteria have been. Depending on the industry, you may find out who your competitors are. See if the list makes any sense. If there are more than three or four names on it, it's probably best to forget about the whole thing.

We are all naturally credulous in our own favour.

Samuel Johnson

Likewise, beware of pitches where the actual mandate is already informally awarded, but where because of purchasing rules several suppliers are approached nevertheless. By the same token, be suspicious of invitations which are not based on a clear top level mandate but seem to be not much more than some junior manager's mall-walking exercise. There is no fool-proof way to detect and avoid these phantom opportunities. The best you can do is to always be cautious when you are approached by a buyer with whom you have never been in any meaningful contact. Chances are he has browsed the web or his meaningless five-hundred-plus social network connections, desperate to come up with sufficient names for his shortlist, and then somehow stumbled upon you or your company's name. When contacted, do a deep drill and ask lots of questions.

Once you have decided to participate in the pitch, stay on guard. All of a sudden you might, for instance, be asked to come up with some preliminary proposals which effectively include work or product that you would normally charge for. You should not comply with such a request. If you are told that one or more competitors supposedly have agreed to do so, that is their problem. Remember that if a prospective customer squeezes you and plays you and your competitors off against each other, he will not cease to do so once he has entrusted some business to you. Are you happy with that prospect?

If money is your hope for independence you will never have it. The only real security that a man will have in this world is a reserve of knowledge, experience, and ability.

HENRY FORD

American car manufacturer and innovator, 1863-1947

At the end of the day, competitive strength is a matter of intellectual rather than monetary or fixed assets. It typically consists of proprietary technology, creative and innovative ability, smart and hard-to-copy business models, customer loyalty and trade relations. Consequently, these assets are the ones which you should protect most keenly against your competitors. Keep them under lock and key, don't expose them in the media because you think it would make for nice company PR and don't put them on the table for some quick, short term gain. Beware of pitches which are nothing but tarnished benchmarking or brain-picking exercises. If you must share any intellectual capital with prospective customers, have them sign a non-disclosure agreement. Finally, remember that suppliers or clients may turn into competitors too (you know, the customer's IT manager who quits to start his own consulting business). So be cautious not to share too much.

25 Managing innovation

In earlier chapters, we discussed the general principles of independent thinking and creativity. Now, let's focus on the more specific domain of innovation. It can be defined as the development of products or services, technologies or processes which do not yet exist and which are more than just spin-offs from existing ones. So, no gradual improvements here. But lots of unpredictability and if all goes well the occasional quantum leap. No guarantees on the latter, though.

There is nothing more difficult to take in hand, more perilous to conduct or more uncertain in its success than to take the lead in the introduction of a new order of things.

NICCOLÒ MACHIAVELLI

If entrepreneurship is risky, entrepreneurship based on innovation is only more so. All major variables are subject to a high degree of uncertainty. Will we be able to design an effective product? Will it survive the reality check in the marketplace? Can we produce it at the right quality level in the necessary numbers? Will we be able to charge prices that allow us to make a profit? Can competitive activity be contained? That's a lot of unpredictability and as a result, the failure rate of innovations is astronomic. That is why it scares the hell out of most people.

He that will not apply new remedies must expect new evils; for time is the greatest innovator.

FRANCIS BACON

Look at any major product or service industry: none of them is in the shape it was in ten to twenty years ago. Markets and technologies have changed dramatically. Innovation is a bare necessity for holding on to your competitive position in the first place, and even more so for growing your business. Even relatively conventional industries full of traditional craftsmanship have experienced plenty of change. Take bespoke clothing. Virtual reality is now used for presentation and measuring, and the internet has become central to the production process. The work in progress may well have travelled the globe before your finished cashmere jacket is delivered at your doorstep. Coming next is robotic sewing, which may turn value chains worldwide upside down once more as they make manual labor less central to the production process. Thus they may put factories in low-wage, faraway countries out of business.

Another example is private investment. Instead of pricey stockbrokers and wealth managers, new web-based platforms offer anybody with a moderate net worth the possibility to invest anytime, anyplace in the global stocks and bonds markets, at a fraction of the usual costs and with results that (certainly net of fees) are often superior.

Innovation is the specific instrument of entrepreneurship: the act that endows resources with a new capacity to create wealth.

PETER DRUCKER

Austrian-born American writer, management consultant and university professor 1909-2005

As an add-on to an existing set of products, innovation can bring you more benefits than just keeping your position in a changing environment. Your pricing and margins may prosper. It's only logical that the best prices can be commanded by new products which offer the buyer unique benefits and which are in some way protected from copycats by, say, tacit production knowledge or patents. This is not to say that you must charge a premium for every innovation. It just means that you have the option to do so, in case you think it makes sense from, for example, a marketing point of view. If your innovations are compelling and can be defended against the competition, it's largely up to you how you would like the market to develop; fast or slow, with aggressive pricing or at premium rates and margins. Indeed, one could say that for a limited amount of time, every innovator is a kind of monopolist with all the usual privileges included.

Our book technology has Gutenberg at one end and the Ford assembly lines at the other. Both are obsolete.

Herbert Marshall McLuhan
Canadian philosopher, 1911-1980

Innovation is only tangible once it's happening. If and how the market will develop is highly unpredictable. As a consequence it's hard to set commercial objectives. Usually, these objectives are too optimistic: the vision, fueled by wishful thinking, travels faster than reality can keep up with. Keep your cool.

We are more ready to try the untried when what we do is inconsequential. Hence the fact that many inventions had their birth as toys.

Eric Hoffer

The innovation process and its results can be disruptive. If you want to give truly innovative products and services a fair chance, you should allow them to develop without influencing, or being influenced by your present day-to-day operations. Potentially great inventions shouldn't be prematurely killed because they are judged and probably rejected by the standards and the people which currently make up your mainstream business. Your existing manufacturing capability, your actual user base or your present distribution network are not necessarily relevant. At the same time, you should keep your present set of winning products (and your crew who works hard at them) from being infected with the novelty virus for its own sake, i.e. without leading to any tangible improvement of its product quality or its bottom line. Ensure that the disruption caused by your innovation hits your competitors rather than your own bread-and-butter business.

Happy the man who early learns the difference between his wishes and his powers.

JOHANN WOLFGANG VON GOETHE

German writer and polymath, 1749-1832

In some businesses, the costs of innovation can be downright prohibitive for smaller players, especially if success is in no way guaranteed even when spending huge amounts. Think of the pharmaceutical industry, where the typical budget for a new medicine is in the hundreds of millions. Such an amount of cash can of course only be found and put at considerable risk by large corporates. This means that in such sectors smaller enterprises are effectively barred from developing innovations. Be certain that your resources are sufficient to play the game in the industry of your choosing.

Innovation has nothing to do with how many R&D dollars you have. When Apple came up with the Mac, IBM was spending at least 100 times more on R&D. It's not about money. It's about the people you have, how you're led, and how much you get it.

Steve Jobs

American technological innovator and entrepreneur, 1955-2011

A company's vast size and resources may actually be a disadvantage. In a smaller, agile company with a culture conducive to innovation, a given amount of money and manpower will take you much further than in a ministry-like environment with its tendency to over-structure, over-analyze and over-scrutinize. Again, if you suspect your main organization to be like this, isolate your innovation department and let them work undisturbed. Of course, once they have come up with something tangible, let them come out and impress even the most conservative forces in your company.

With engineering, I view this year's failure as next year's opportunity to try it again. Failures are not something to be avoided. You want to have them happen as quickly as you can so you can make progress rapidly.

GORDON MOORE

American information technology scientist and entrepreneur, 1929

If the principle of trial and error ever applies, it is with innovation. After all, finding out what doesn't work is a way to find out what does. At the same time, speed is of the essence. There is always the risk that a competitor is working on the same inventions as you are. Remember, the good old gramophone disc, which in its time was a clear innovation too, was invented more or less simultaneously in at least three different places over the world. Chances are that you are not the only one busy with failing forward to a certain new discovery. Again, as they say in Silicon Valley: 'Make your mistakes, but make them in a hurry.'

Every man I meet is in some way my superior; and in that I can learn of him.

RALPH WALDO EMERSON

Although it may seem counter-intuitive, innovation is a people's business more than anything else. Picking the right brains right from the start, be it from scientists, potential customers, trade parties or other opinion leaders, can put you on the right track faster and more accurately than going it alone and burying yourself into piles of research. So have you and your innovations team go out a lot. When exchanging ideas with thought leaders, you will get valuable feedback on every subject, whether it's design, production or marketing. You may also want to use their expertise to do a more focused, more effective research effort. It helps tremendously if you know where to look and equally importantly where not to look.

Take the advice of a faithful friend, and submit thy inventions to his censure.

THOMAS FULLER

English churchman and historian, 1608-1661

We have already stressed the importance of talking and listening to your supporters. They are especially valuable when the stakes are high and uncertainty abounds, as is the case with innovation. Ideally, your supporter base should include some professionals from the industrial and scientific community relevant to your innovation. But don't forget to add some independent thinkers who are not bothered by such background and in-depth knowledge and who offer some common sense practical help as well.

26 Managing quality

Here goes for another job that is both demanding and never done: managing quality. Yet, as with many other demanding and ongoing jobs like raising and educating children, the long-term rewards that come with them are considerable. Offering quality will bring you a string of sustainable benefits, ranging from loyal customers and tasty margins to job satisfaction for yourself and for everybody employed at your company.

It takes less time to do a thing right than it does to explain why you did it wrong.

HENRY WADSWORTH LONGFELLOW

American poet, 1807-1882

Some people think that they cannot afford to offer quality. They obviously never had to recall cars with airbag defects, reprint brochures with type errors in them or offer free meals to dissatisfied guests in their restaurant. Neither did they ever have to defend themselves in endless lawsuits because of damages created by faulty products. Instead of considering whether you can afford to offer genuine quality, ask yourself whether you can afford not to.

Quality is a direct experience independent of and prior to intellectual abstractions.

ROBERT M. PIRSIG
American philosopher and novelist, 1928

Ever listened to a well-produced Bach or Steely Dan record on a headphone which produced crystal-clear sound and which was beautifully finished in every detail, up to the soft, supple leather cushions cuddling up to your ears? Ever driven a car which offered great road handling and was an understated stunner to look at from any angle? Ever worn a suit which was so light and cut to the bone you forgot you were wearing one? In all of these cases you have recognized and enjoyed quality without the use of hard criteria or whatever metric scale. You experienced it as a whole, for many reasons great and small. That's the magic of quality.

One cannot develop taste from what is of average quality but only from the very best.

GOETHE

Indeed, you could argue that a top quality product or service even has the ability to change people's minds about the product category. Many people who think they're not into wine revise their opinion once they have tasted a great Bordeaux. Others, who have never been keen on cars, change their mind once they have been at the wheel of an excellent piece of German automotive engineering. In other words, offering top quality is the way forward if you want to engage in market creation.

Beware of the man who won't be bothered with details.

William A. Feather

American publisher and author, 1889-1981

As to the process, quality management consists of many small routine checks which must be done over and over again. Every detail counts. Imagine you have just rented a car, topped up with fuel and freshly washed. So far so good, and off you go. Once you have hit the road, however, it turns out that the windscreen washer fluid tank is empty. Trivial as it may seem, this slight neglect will surely have deteriorated the over-all quality impression of the car rental company in your mind. With quality the beauty, as well as the devil, is in the details.

Likewise, improvement in quality also consists of small achievements. The process will be a steady one rather than one of sudden quantum leaps after prolonged periods of seemingly fruitless stagnation, as tends to be the case with innovation.

The best is the enemy of the good.

VOLTAIRE

Of course, all these little yet important facets of quality make for a process which is characterized by a lot of discipline and a relentless drive for perfectionism. That is the reason for all those thick, continuously improved and updated production manuals, service guidelines and checklists. Ensuring an output of constant, ever higher quality has a touch of single-minded army drill to it. Chances are that you, being an entrepreneur, are not good at this. Be sure you have people on board who are.

Quality means doing it right when no one is looking.

HENRY FORD

At the same time, all the manuals and boot camps in the world cannot make infallible, zero-defect robots out of the human beings who do the actual work. There are limits to the extent you can control them during the process. What's more, faulty work tends to reveal itself at an unpredictable moment, often only sometime after the product has left your premises. Even a sorry pair of shoes looks okay the first few weeks of wearing them, before they quickly and finally lose shape and luster. Most cars do alright the first few years before a lousy paint job starts showing. Buildings and bridges which have been poorly constructed don't tumble down immediately upon their completion. Thus, this usually delayed exposure of poor quality further impedes the effective control you have. Your best chance of detecting a badly done job is when it's already too late.

So the quest for quality always involves trust and mutual regard between you and your customers and also between you and your work force. At the end of the day, you must rely on every individual employee assuming his or her own responsibilities. The best way to ensure quality is to ensure that everybody at your organization has an autonomous drive and an innate pleasure to pursue it. It helps, of course, if you provide the right incentives too. Don't overload your staff with work, be sure to provide them with the right tools, pay them well, praise them for a job particularly well done and have them use the company's products and services on favorable terms. If all that is lacking, the thickest HowTo will be utterly useless.

Every job is a self-portrait of the person who does it.
Autograph your work with excellence.

AUTHOR UNKNOWN

Especially in service businesses, it's the people who make the difference. Just think of your last air trip. The plane may have been full. The flight may have been delayed as a result of air traffic control. The food may have been classically horrible. Yet, the cabin crew probably had a big impact on your total experience. Did they treat you with genuine hospitality and bring the various pieces of bad news with a halfway authentic smile? This probably alleviated if not compensated that awkward, narrow seat, that stressful reshuffling of your schedule or that ghastly bun with its E number specs on the wrapper. The friendly flight attendant will be remembered long after these nuisances have been forgotten.

In construction too, individual craftsmanship makes a difference and is to be honored. For years, the British sports car manufacturer Aston Martin added a small brass shield on every finished engine with the name of the head mechanic who had been in charge of its assembly. That's a nice gesture, both to the mechanic and to the customer. Be sure that your employees and their work are individually recognized as much as possible, even if the production process is highly structured. Make them proud of their achievements. Share customer feedback with them. Be sure to reward great performance with the right words and the right gestures.

27 Marketing

No matter how sound your offer happens to be, the product which nobody knows or cares about stands no chance of getting sold. Whether you like it or not, you must do marketing. This basically means offering your product at the right price, the right place and with the right selling message. The marketing profession as such is not an academic science but a minor art, just like entrepreneurship. This means that there are no golden recipes and that successes are often not repeatable. Inevitably you will waste both time and money, but not spending any of either on marketing will ultimately cost you more. Test your programs as much as possible: use pilot stores, send test mailings to smaller groups, do local price promotions, run regional ad campaigns.

Marketing is what you do when your product is no good.

EDWIN H. LAND

American scientist and inventor, 1909-1991

Many entrepreneurs are so fond of their product, they silently resent the idea that it would benefit from any commercial support. But unless you have found a once-in-a-century breakthrough medical cure for a lethal disease, you cannot trust your product to sell itself without any marketing support. Paradoxically, even in case of groundbreaking innovative products you need a solid marketing strategy to overcome probable barriers. Think of fixed ideas and established patterns of use in the customer's mind, about present opinion leader views, defensive moves from competitors who'd like things to stay as they are, conservative distribution channels with their existing flow of goods and other aspects of the status quo which you are about to challenge. You need a clever pricing strategy, a compelling sales message and a sound distribution plan to enhance your chance of success.

Tell me and I forget, teach me and I may remember, involve me and I learn.

Benjamin Franklin (attributed)

The more interactive your marketing is, the more effective it will be. Whenever possible, offer mass customization. Would you like your dress to be a little longer or without a split? No problem. A double portion of garlic on your pizza? Of course. A free test drive of the accounting app with some of your own figures as input? Go ahead. Make various pricing offers and let your customer choose which one is the best fit. Include tests on your website which assist your buyers in making the right choice. Add personal home pages where they can store their preferences for future buying. Create or encourage customer forums for continuous improvement of your products and services. In other words, actively involve your customers whenever possible throughout the total cycle: when they are still a prospect, when they buy, when they use and when they are up for a repeat purchase.

Price is what you pay. Value is what you get.

Warren Buffett

American investor, 1930

What you can and should charge for your spicy dress, pizza or accounting app is largely up to you. The key factor to consider when setting your price is what your offer is worth to your customers. This value may not bear any relation to the costs you had to incur to produce it. It may be much higher, in which case you will make a lot of money, until of course competition catches up. It may be much lower, in which case you will find it tough to make any profit at all. Remember that many entrepreneurs focus too much on a cost-plus approach. They calculate the price they should ask based on the expenses they make, add a healthy profit margin to these costs: and presto. As a result, they may charge too little and leave money on the table. Conversely, they may discover that they will not be able to run a healthy business in the first place because they cannot sell at prices which would enable them to make any profit. In short: go about pricing with an open mind and firstly, listen without prejudice to what the market is telling you.

Labour was the first price, the original purchase – money that was paid for all things. It was neither by gold nor by silver but by labour that all wealth of the world was originally purchased.

Adam Smith

In order to keep a realistic view on what to charge for your products, place yourself in your customers' shoes and do the same math which they probably do themselves. How much work do I have to do, or how much business do I have to generate myself in order to be able to buy that object or that service? Is it okay with me to work a full day for that dress? Work two hours for that restaurant meal? Sell a thousand euros worth of merchandise at low margins so that I can buy this app?
Even if you are catering to large corporates, do the same type of calculations on their part.

What we obtain too cheap, we esteem too lightly: it is dearness only that gives every thing its value.

THOMAS PAINE
English-American political writer, theorist and activist, 1737-1809

Unless you have a great competitive advantage as a large-scale, low-cost supplier selling a commodity-type of product, you should avoid selling based on price. It is usually bad for customer loyalty: there will always emerge another competitor undercutting you on price and if this was your prime selling argument you will be substituted without much hesitation. Selling on price is also bad for your margins, and thus for your profitability, and thus for your options to re-invest in quality and service. So selling on price now will force you to sell on price down the road. It's a vicious circle that can be hard to break out of.

Worse, rock bottom pricing might not even help you get or keep customers. Low prices tend to create mistrust. To the prospective customer, they are a motivation to find fault with what you have to offer and to look elsewhere. Your actually converted customer will also find these low prices cold comfort once the actual experience of using your products (on the quality of which you were forced to economize) turns out to be below par. Sooner rather than later he will switch to a competitor, happy to pay a few dollars more, saying that he knew all along how stupid it was just to look for the cheapest offer.

Advertise your business. Do not hide your light under a bushel.

P.T. Barnum

American showman and circus founder, 1810-1891

As an entrepreneur, you are intensely involved with your product day after day, from nine to five and probably beyond. It can thus be difficult to realize that this same product may not be the most important thing in the life of your customers. As a rule, you will overestimate to what extent these very customers are aware of your company, your brand and your products in the first place. Likewise for their interest, appreciation and loyalty. So you probably have to talk to your customers more often than you'd think would be necessary to drive home the essentials of your offer. You also have to be more simple and repetitive in your messages than you're probably inclined to be. It is an old saying in advertising circles that a campaign starts to become genuinely effective when the client and the agency have already been fed up with it for quite a while.

We hear only half of what is said to us, understand only half of that, believe only half of that, and remember only half of that.

MIGNON MCLAUGHLIN

American journalist and author, 1913-1983

Even if the target group's interest in what you have to offer is apparent and they are fully tuned to what you have to say, you should take note of the limitations of the human mind. Have you ever sat around a camp fire with some friends and played the game in which you had to tell your neighbor on your right a certain simple story, which he in turn had to pass on to his neighbor, and so on until the story had come full circle? Typically, the original text had undergone hilarious changes under way. The simpler you keep your messages, the smaller the chance of bias.

Whatever is common is despised. Advertisements are now so numerous that they are very negligently perused, and it is therefore become necessary to gain attention by magnificence of promises and by eloquence, sometimes sublime and sometimes pathetic.

SAMUEL JOHNSON

Given the plethora of promotional messages anytime anywhere, you are in a constant battle for your target group's attention. It is imperative to stand out, but that is the easy part. To stand out and yet to be appealing and relevant is a more difficult thing. Most difficult, though, is to pull this off for a longer period of time. It's like having a store or publishing a magazine. Starting one up is the easiest thing in the world, keeping it afloat is the biggest challenge imaginable. All the time, you will have to balance between change and stability, practicing the fine art of keeping things sparkling and fresh while at the same time establishing a durable identity for your product and brand that people can relate to over time.

Remove everything that has no relevance to the story. If you say in the first chapter that there is a rifle hanging on the wall, in the second or third chapter it absolutely must go off. If it's not going to be fired, it shouldn't be hanging there.

ANTON CHEKHOV

Russian physician, playwright and author, 1860-1904

A good sales pitch, webpage or print advertisement should have no loose ends. Every word, every visual detail must be geared to the ultimate key response you would like to generate. Don't try to be all things to all men and don't squeeze too many different messages into one. If your new app has eight great features, don't be lazy: think hard to reshape and restate them as one main advantage. If that really isn't possible, focus on the strongest selling point and be confident that your audience will create a broader positive view around it by themselves. Do as the car manufacturer BMW has done for decades with its *Freude am Fahren* slogan, which is a clear, convincing choice for one strong customer benefit (driving pleasure) and suggestive of many others at the same time.

A great ad campaign will make a bad product fail faster. It will get more people to know it's bad.

Bill Bernbach

American advertising executive, 1911-1982

A final word of caution. Marketing is not a panacea. It is a misunderstanding that it would enable you to cover up a foul product. Certainly in this era of interactive social media, the opposite is more likely. Bad customer experiences are bleeped into the world at large without ado and in a split second. Your own social network pages can become tainted in no time. And the more well-known and esteemed your company or brand happens to be, the more vulnerable you are. Avoid creating false impressions and thus expectations with your campaign which in reality will not be met. Be careful what you claim. And, of course, always deliver products and services as if the whole world were watching, which it actually is. More about that in the next chapter.

28 Reputation

Obtaining and holding on to a good reputation is something akin to making and preserving really good money: there is no sure-fire way to do it. So, as with all things beyond your control, a good reputation should be considered a side-effect of what you're doing rather than your primary goal. The best way to work on your reputation is probably not to pay too much dedicated attention. Just be certain to have you and your crew act in such a way that it fills you with pride or at least respect at all times.

A good reputation is more valuable than money.

PUBLILIUS SYRUS

A good reputation can make you extra money in a fairly effortless manner. A favorable review, a few positive references, they may go a long way towards bringing you new business without much investment or acquisition. A good reputation may also enable you to hold on to existing customers on favorable terms and to enjoy an ever growing fan base who will create further positive spin. People like to associate with well-regarded individuals and parties. But it doesn't work the other way around. Spending a lot of money on the improvement of your reputation may actually have a counterproductive effect. People will think that you're trying too hard and will start questioning your motives. Money can't buy reputation. What's more: monetary setbacks, unpleasant as they may be, are easier to recover from than reputational ones. The latter are often beyond repair at any price. Just ask any fired CEO or blackballed politician.

Whenever you do a thing, act as if all the world were watching.

THOMAS JEFFERSON

Co-founder and president of the United States, 1743-1826

To the extent that you can influence it, safeguarding your reputation is a matter of avoiding mistakes, of not blowing it, rather than about doing the right thing. This is counterintuitive to the trial-and-error mindset of an entrepreneur, so take care. As a safety valve, whenever you are considering a course of action of which you are not entirely sure, pause and imagine what your supporters would say. Better still, change the course of action altogether as soon as any doubt emerges.

Talking much about oneself can also be a means to conceal oneself.

FRIEDRICH NIETZSCHE

Though maximum transparency is generally regarded a good thing for companies to pursue these days, the way to keep up a good reputation includes knowing what not to disclose. This is not because you would have anything improper to hide, but because excessive, unsolicited disclosure of everything you think and every detailed step you and your company take will not resonate well with the outside world. People may get confused or bored by you. You may create an impression of insecurity and weakness. You may also raise needless suspicion.

Associate yourself with men of good quality if you esteem your own reputation, for 'tis better to be alone than in bad company.

GEORGE WASHINGTON (ATTRIBUTED)

Co-founder and first president of the United States, 1732-1799

To a large extent, your standing in the business world depends on the prominence or otherwise of the individuals with whom you team up. Whether you like it or not, others will judge you by the relations you have. It is a way for people who do not know you that well to assess you. Their opinion of you will closely resemble the opinion they will have of your peer group. Obviously, this risk-reducing move on their part adds to the lack of control on yours. After all, you can never know for sure how your partners and other close associates will behave over time, what skeletons are still hiding in their closets and how possible future troubles they'll get themselves into will rub off on you. Again, it is wise to stay on the safe side. Look at the connections people have when you want to relate to them. Don't ever make the mistake of entering any kind of association with persons who you do not feel entirely comfortable about, just for the sake of cooperation. If you have some reservations about someone, and don't like their entourage, it usually proves to be for good reason. Don't succumb to destructive optimism. People don't change. And you are who you know.

We suppress in ourselves that which we are really good at in order to adapt to the opinion of the public. What we really are, in real life, we consider less important than the impression we make.

MICHEL DE MONTAIGNE

An obsession with your reputation will make you less original and less daring in your ventures. Accept that you cannot be all things to all men. Can you name one famous businessman or businesswoman who is universally admired? There will always be persons who won't like you, your company or your products. That's the way it is. Don't try to please everybody lest you end up pleasing nobody, yourself included.

Public opinion is a jurisdiction that no honorable man will ever completely accept but never completely reject.

Sébastien-Roch Nicolas (Chamfort)
French playwright and writer, 1741-1794

All in all, it is a mistake to overestimate the importance of reputation, but a bigger mistake to ignore the topic altogether. Facilitate good things to happen by keeping up the good work as you see fit, enjoy your possible hard-earned prestige in moderation without getting intoxicated and don't challenge fate by taking unnecessary risks.

29 Cost control

Since business is about making money, the importance of controlling costs is secondary only to the importance of creating revenues. One of the more difficult jobs for any entrepreneur is to decide upon the right expenditure: spend too much, or on the wrong kind of things, and you will go under. Spend too little and the same may happen. There is no such thing as the right way of spending, or the right amount. If you are in a more or less established industry, general ratios may be available which tell you whether you are in line with your peers. There may also be reasons why your company is atypical, of course. Be that as it may, but whenever you are about to incur any significant cost by acquiring or hiring anybody or anything, be certain that your decision-making is well-balanced. Consider both the costs and the benefits, the risks and the returns. Avoid buying on a whim as well as falling victim to undue stinginess; this summarizes the approach of the homo economicus which is key to successful entrepreneurship.

Spare not, nor spend too much, be this thy care, Spare but to spend, and only spend to spare. Who spends too much may want, and so complain. But he spends best that spares to spend again.

THOMAS RANDOLPH

English poet and dramatist, 1605-1635

The entrepreneur's game is to invest, generate a profit and reinvest again. So he's neither a big saver nor a big spender by nature. Rather, he is continuously synthesizing these two qualities into an investor's approach. Money must be employed, i.e. put to use in a profitable manner, instead of put into coma by hoarding or burnt by consuming. All capital outlays must serve a business purpose. All business activity must lead to profitability and further growth of capital, ready to be put back in circulation again for new business purposes and new profits, and so on. Consumption or mere preservation of capital is regarded as equal to missing opportunities. All this is not a matter of insatiability on the entrepreneur's part. It's all about the eternal love of creating value.

A fool and his money are soon parted.

GEORGE BUCHANAN

Scottish historian and humanist scholar, 1506-1582

Whenever substantial costs are about to be incurred,

the entrepreneur should first ask himself a couple of tough questions. Can I afford this expenditure in the first place? What is the envisaged outcome of this capital outlay? Lower total costs? Higher productivity? A better product? Happier customers? Higher sales? How likely is that outcome? How unique is the offer I'm about to pay good money for? Have I shopped around? How is the value-for-money developing for this product or service category in general? Might I get a better deal in six months' time? Have others been buying lately and what is their experience? For how long do I need to commit myself when buying? Will I be able to afford the costs down the road? Will the expenditure be of the sunk cost type or is there any re-sale value? Which two or three alternatives could the money be spent on instead? Smart buying is essential to being a successful entrepreneur.

Expenditures rise to meet income.

C. Northcote Parkinson

It is easier to define whether or not you can afford something than whether you need it in the first place. But intelligent dealing with the latter question may lead to massive savings and a less complicated life. So in order to manage costs well, you not only need a knock for numbers but also an independent mind. Avoid herd behavior ("Let's buy this new software; everybody else does."). Also, avoid buying goods and services because you think that they fit your increased scale of operations. Do you really need that receptionist, that secretary, that full-time bookkeeper, that glitzy but fast-depreciating executive car? Will those power lunches, those trade fair visits around the globe and those coveted club memberships bring in new business? Or will they just fondle your ego?

It requires a very unusual mind to undertake the analysis of the obvious.

ALFRED NORTH WHITEHEAD
English mathematician and philosopher, 1861-1947

Next to judging any new capital expenditure along the lines mentioned above, you should also screen your existing expenses on a regular basis. This is especially important if your business has experienced strong growth. Under these circumstances, cost items which have been in the books for a while are probably accepted and paid for on autopilot. There seems no time and not much need to dive into them. But they may add up all the same and there may be outdated products and services among them. Be like an intelligent investor who monitors his securities at regular intervals, asking himself each time whether he would buy each individual stock again if it weren't in the portfolio already. In other words, have a periodical screening of all expenses. Assess every one of them as if you were buying the related product or service for the very first time. Look at your software subscriptions, your caterer, your accountants: would you hire them again if you were to start all over today? Are they still the best choice? Do they still offer the best value-for-money in the market? Based on the here and now, you may well decide to cut down some habit-driven or conformity-driven expenditures and to initiate or step up others.

The cost of a thing is the amount of what I call life which is required to be exchanged for it, immediately or in the long run.

HENRY DAVID THOREAU

Nothing comes for free. Never forget that the money now available to you for spending on any good or service has been earned at the earlier expense of precious time and energy on your part. But the sacrifice does not stop there. Each new cost center requires more resources than the purchase price alone. Whenever you install a new machine, appoint a new employee or hire an external advisor, you should be prepared to add time, money and mental capacity for maintenance and supervision to the cost. These are often neglected, as they usually do not come with a neat, separate invoice. But they add up nevertheless. Your bookkeeper needs to spend time on the administration of your company car; your office manager needs to pay attention to the new receptionist; you and your top management have to commit time, money and brainpower to the management of your external consultants if you want to extract maximum value out of them. In all of these cases, managing a product or service requires more scarce resources than you'll see on the supplier's original bill or on the hired hand's pay slip.

Sometimes, these additional costs turn out to overshadow the benefits for which the goods or services were bought in the first place, like a holiday trip which makes you return to the office worn-out instead of refreshed. There are distractive employees who make costly mistakes and who drain energy from everybody they work with. There are new computer programs the use of which creates more headaches than their benefits could possibly justify. There are copywriters whose texts you have to spend more time correcting than if you'd written the piece yourself. In all of these cases, you should have sent rather than received a bill, though financial compensation only goes so far when making up for the loss of precious time.

Lost wealth may be replaced by industry, lost knowledge by study, lost health by temperance or medicine, but lost time is gone forever.

SAMUEL SMILES

Scottish author and reformer, 1812-1904

When considering the total of obligations related to

owning any good or service, wasting money may indeed be the least of your worries. By comparison, the waste of time is less reversible and therefore much more critical. So avoid buying yourself into dependence and ultimately poverty by spending all your time and intelligence on people or stuff which were supposed to help you create value but in practice only detract you from doing so and effectively drain your resources.

Luxury: The lust for comfort, that stealthy thing that enters the house as a guest, and then becomes a host, and then a master.

KHALIL GIBRAN

Lebanese artist, poet and writer, 1883-1931

Luxury weakens the entrepreneurial spirit. Think of that infamous high-fashion internet startup which burned millions of dollars every month, without a penny of actual sales materializing. Its founders continued to travel the world by Concorde until the very end, when the funding dried up and the whole venture collapsed. Or think of academic studies like the one by Liu and Yermack which prove that the performance of listed companies deteriorates when its CEOs acquire extremely large or costly mansions and estates. Apparently, there is a price to pay for conspicuous consumption, whether the money is available or not. It's not about money. It's about mental focus. Unproductive expenditure is the beginning of the entrepreneurial end.

Economy is the art of making the most of life. The love of economy is the root of all virtue.

George Bernard Shaw

A totally different reason for constantly scrutinizing costs is that the prices and the relative value-for-money offered by each product type may change. Consider some long term price developments. Costs of cell phones, computer power, cars and air travel have come down. Costs of personally provided services (doctors, secretaries, waiters, stage performers, consultants) have gone up, both in absolute and in relative terms. This is because the practitioners cannot leverage themselves and do not accomplish productivity gains like those attained in technological and manufacturing circles. As a result their services tend to become comparatively unaffordable over time. This phenomenon is known as Baumol's disease.

With the help of books, education formats, web-based services and plug-and-play technologies, many former expert jobs can today be done in part or even in full by yourself, at no or low out-of-pocket expense. Think of advertising, photography, accounting, money management, psychological coaching, travel booking, basic legal counselling, recruiting and yes, sometimes even entrepreneurial advice!

Then there are prices which fluctuate according to supply and demand. Examples include housing, commodities and money itself, of course. Always keep a keen eye on what's on offer at what prices today and keep adjusting your purchasing accordingly.

Frugality should ever be practised but not excessive parsimony.

HITOPADESA

While immersing ourselves in all this economizing, it should still be noted that there is a difference between smart buying and minimizing costs no matter what. Don't overdo it on austerity lest it may have a counter-productive effect. That old, battered, fully depreciated car may leave you standing in the emergency lane sooner or later, possibly when you happen to be heading to that important meeting with a client (and probably when it's raining). The twenty dollar premium you choose not to pay for a seat with extra leg room will rob you of two hours of extra comfort and productive work during your next budget flight. Serving bad coffee at your office will surely save you a few dollars per employee per month, but the costs in terms of daily dismay and a worsened working climate are hard to quantify but will certainly be much higher.

If you pay peanuts, you get monkeys.

James Goldsmith

Anglo-French financier and politician, 1933-1997

With salaries being the biggest expense for most businesses, it is tempting to economize on them as much as possible. Certainly in times of recession and unemployment you may be able to hire at moderated wages. But with the right breed of professional workers, this will cause bad blood. Though their personal circumstances may force them to agree to your penny-pinching proposal, they will feel being taken advantage of. Inevitably their motivation and performance will suffer and they will quit again at the earliest opportunity. Just remember that in the long run, you get what you pay for. Would you rather spend five thousand a month on a splendid account manager who delights your customers, or three and a half grand on an unremarkable one? Which of the two options is the most expensive at the end of the day?

Penny wise, pound foolish.

Robert Burton

English scholar, 1577-1640

Some people go out of their way bending paperclips back into their original shape, using the back side of photocopies as note paper and switching off the lights in their office whenever they move away from their desk for just a few minutes. Curiously, they may well be the same people who think nothing of spending megabucks on last minute, full-fare flight tickets for meetings where they cannot be missed, or so they like to think. Especially travel expenses are often dealt with as if they weren't actual costs. The same is for restaurant costs, seminar costs and other expenses which have an ego-enhancing quality and a touch of dynamism and worldliness to them.

The habitually punctual make all their mistakes right on time.

LAURENCE J. PETER
Canadian educator, 1919-1990

You can observe the same phenomenon when it comes to spending time. Many people put great value on having regular meetings which are also supposed to start dead on time, allowing for no delay whatsoever. It is of no relevance to them that these meetings may be utterly unproductive as enough comfort is derived from the regularity and the punctuality. For good measure, the same meeting addicts may also dole out impressive To Do lists as a legitimation of the next event – where valuable, scarce resources will be wasted again. As an entrepreneur, you should be wary of this false sense of efficiency. Minimize the number of regular meetings as well as their duration.

Too many people spend money they haven't earned to buy things they don't want to impress people they don't like.

WILL ROGERS
American humorist, 1879-1935

Paying too much attention to what other people think quickly leads to incurring unnecessary costs in order to get by. Before you know it, you drive a car you cannot afford, occupy an office building which whispers that your prices are too high, and overspend on the very latest smartphone because you don't want to be caught with an outdated model. Again, controlling costs requires an independent spirit. The people you'd like to respect you will do so irrespective of the status symbols you've gathered around you. People who don't and who you'd like to teach a lesson by flashing around your possessions are not worth bothering about in the first place, nor are they a worthy cause of useless spending on your part.

I'd like to live as a poor man with lots of money.

PABLO PICASSO (ATTRIBUTED)
Spanish artist, 1881-1973

Ever been in the situation where you made a nice bit of unexpected surplus money, walked into a car dealership on impulse and suddenly found yourself without any further interest to buy? Congratulations, your ego was strengthened in a way no spending could ever achieve. If you're mentally healthy, you do not need the narcotics of consumption or prestige. Spend and save your time and money accordingly. Your person and your balance sheet will gain strength with every forfeited purchase.

The comfy Eames chair, the good copper pans, the '54 Strat: these are the things I miss the most.

WALTER BECKER & DONALD FAGEN
American jazz rock musicians, founders and core members of the band Steely Dan, 1950 (Becker), 1948 (Fagen)

Of course, the temptation to obtain well-made stuff may still rear its head every now and then. There is nothing wrong with that. Just ensure that when buying, you are propelled by the right motive. To paraphrase an earlier quote, quality is not only what you do when nobody is looking. Quality is also what you prefer to use irrespective of whether others are around or not. Do you really think that this new, slick notebook PC rather than being a must-have because all tech investors suddenly seem to have one, lets you or your crew do a better job with more ease and higher productivity? Then go ahead and by all means get it.

I have turned my entire attention to Greek. The first thing I shall do, as soon as the money arrives, is to buy some Greek authors; after that, I shall buy clothes.

Desiderius Erasmus

All in all, when ranking your purchasing priorities, always put the things first which offer the highest return over time. Viewed that way, expenditure on further development of knowledge in the broadest sense, and thus of the intellectual capital of your organization, must prevail over any other buying at all times. Whether this knowledge transfer is in printed, online or personal form, spend as much as you can on making your organization smarter every day. The gratification may be delayed compared to other alternatives, but it will be bigger in the end.

30 Business ethics & the law

Entrepreneurship as such knows no ethics and is a-moral. Like money and sex, it is a force which is neither good nor bad; it is beyond virtue or vice. That is why you can't start an ethical, legally compliant enterprise. These qualities are at best conditions, but they are never at the core of a business. Of course these very conditions are important all the same. Entrepreneurship is a potentially positive force which has a proven power to improve the well-being of humanity through better products and increased economic activity and wealth. Yet it may also do outright harm to individuals or to society. Moreover, the world of business is strife with conflicts of interest, notably in the shape of battles for scarce resources (capital, goods, talent, markets). All in all, ethics and law are important safety valves when it comes to a more or less orderly deployment of capitalism and its gung-ho offspring, entrepreneurship.

To streamline the subject in accordance with the compact set-up of this book, I first propose three pragmatic, overall principles to adhere to and on which this chapter is built.

First, business in general, entrepreneurship included, should do no outright harm to anybody or anything (with a tip of the hat to Hippocrates). Second, conflicts of interest in an entrepreneurial environment should be resolved in a way which

presupposes that in business conflicts in general, no single party in the conflict is likely to ever be fully and exclusively in the right. This principle is in turn based on the assumption that in a basically a-moral environment, it is impossible to define right or wrong in absolute terms. Third, if you as an entrepreneur can identify with these two axioms, you are thereby encouraged to go by your own conscience and fair judgment in every situation.

Some people regard private enterprise as a predatory tiger to be shot. Others look on it as a cow they can milk. Not enough people see it as a healthy horse, pulling a sturdy wagon.

WINSTON CHURCHILL
British statesman and prime minister of the United Kingdom, historian, writer and artist, 1874-1965

Although capitalism and entrepreneurship are not able to create a just society all by themselves, they may nevertheless act as catalysts. And you can be part of that. By offering sound and possibly innovative products at decent prices, by paying employees fair wages and by paying a reasonable amount of taxes in the countries where the economic value is actually created.

More and more I have come to the conclusion that a principle isn't a principle until it costs you money.

BILL BERNBACH

Aiming for the highest degree of ethics in business is admirable, but there is often a price to pay. Products which qualify as environmentally friendly or which are produced according to standards of fair trade may be of lower quality; they may also cost more than others. Clean tech production methods may be economically unattractive. Paying wages which are substantially above industry standards may deteriorate your competitive position. In all of these cases there are trade-offs to make.

Avoid putting yourself out of business by raising the bar too high. Do well by doing good whenever you reasonably can, but only then. And don't go it alone. See which parties can be mobilized throughout the value chain to share the costs involved with doing business the right way. Let all of them put their money where their mouth is. Have customers pay a little more for products with a sustainable character. Have trade partners accept a little less margin on sales. Find out what government subsidies or tax redemptions are possible. Accept a little less return on capital yourself, maybe.

It is not, what a lawyer tells me I may do; but what humanity, reason, and justice, tell me I ought to do.

EDMUND BURKE

In a mundane environment like the world of the entrepreneur, it may be tempting to fully concentrate on the legal side of things. This would mean that you, for instance, would think nothing of making a living by tricking money out of people with slot machines as long as there is no law against doing so. Or talking somebody into buying a house or a car which you clearly sense he can ill afford. Or drawing your employees rosy career perspectives which you know damn well are not feasible, just to make them swallow their current modest paycheck. A mature entrepreneur will never only consider what he could get away with from a strictly legal point of view. He will put too much of himself in everything he does to engage in lowlife pursuits or to exploit any of his company's stakeholders, irrespective of legal backing.

The court bows to the lessons of experience and the force of better reasoning, recognizing that the process of trial and error, so fruitful in the physical sciences, is appropriate also in the judicial function.

LOUIS D. BRANDEIS

American lawyer and associate justice on the Supreme Court, 1856-1941

Just as the wisest of doctors are the first to admit that the medical knowledge of today will be outdated tomorrow, the most thoughtful legal professionals are quick to acknowledge that no law nor any application of it should ever be carved in stone. Consequently, blind obedience to the law is less appropriate than well-considered compliance. This certainly holds true for you as an entrepreneur. After all, you will venture into no man's land more often than the average person. You may therefore experience situations in which the boundaries of present legislation are tested. It is imaginable that you will find yourself not only at the frontier of societal developments, but also in jurisprudence. The more innovative your products, your business model or your patterns of cooperation and dealing, the more likely it is for you to enter legal terra incognita. The good news is that you may be able to manoeuver relatively freely, without suffocating regulation. The bad news is that you may not know some roadblocks until they materialize. It may be a choppy ride involving considerable amounts of time and money.

Avoid lawsuits beyond all things; they pervert your conscience, impair your health, and dissipate your property.

JEAN DE LA BRUYÈRE

The same principle we discussed in the chapter about competition applies again. All efforts you dedicate to legal matters cannot be geared to delighting your customers or to other equally productive goals. Before you know it, being immersed in lawsuits will fully occupy your mind. You will think and talk about not much else from breakfast at the kitchen table to bringing your children to bed at night. Even if you think you are in the right, consider the costs of this mental blockade. Add what you think are the likely legal fees. Double them. Project the damages you think you are entitled to. Cut them in half. Find out what the other guy's funding of legal costs looks like. Is he an entrepreneur just like you? Is your opponent a large corporation with deep pockets, where nobody bears the costs individually and which probably has more dry powder than you do? Do they have in-house counsel? Are they likely to be insured against legal costs? And finally, could it be that maybe, just maybe, they too have a case? Remember the premise we agreed upon about absolute right and wrong being hard to assess in business conflicts in general. Do your analysis. Then see if your case is still worth pursuing.

When you're fighting a case, if you have the facts on your side hammer them into the jury. And if you have the law on your side hammer it into the judge. If you have neither the facts nor the law, hammer hell into the table.

UNKNOWN LAW PROFESSOR

When, at some point, you find yourself in legal procedures all the same, remember that you may use the law, the facts or whatever rhetorical tactic you and your lawyer may have up your sleeve to get what you want. Don't be overly prudent and don't hesitate to use all three as you and your counsel see fit. Your opponent will do exactly the same. Though you may strive for harmony in relations with your fellow men in general, the fact that you are in court indicates that this option is suspended for the moment. Better to accept this and act accordingly or else you will be taken to the cleaners.

Once you've made up your mind to frequent only men capable of acting honestly, ethically, reasonably and truthfully towards you, men who view convention, vanity and etiquette as merely means to bolster up society, then this decision will be likely to result in your having to live more or less on your own.

CHAMFORT

Whether you have emerged as a winner or not, or

whether a fair settlement has been reached or not, court cases are sobering experiences. Perhaps people you got along with in earlier times have suddenly revealed a new, previously unknown greedy, inconsiderate or revengeful side. Or you may have found it hard to swallow that your opponent had a better case, or did a better job at presenting it. Rest assured that an ill-obtained victory will ultimately leave a bad taste in any reasonable person's mouth.

It may be that your experiences in the arena of ethical or legal disputes lead to a downward readjustment of your opinion about some of your relations, or about mankind in general. But even if you have valid reasons for disappointment, don't withdraw into a recluse. Don't condemn the human race, yourself possibly included. Remember the impossibility of defining absolute right and wrong in a business environment in the first place. Also, think of what this dentist once said: 'I have people in my chair all day, but nobody is himself or herself under the circumstances. I do not get to know the real persons. I am basically alone all of the time.' The courtroom has a similar effect. Most people hate it, or at least find themselves unaccustomed to the environment. Some may afterwards regret their behavior there. They may have been driven by uncertainty or fear. They may have been intimidated by their boss or by any other person or entity whom they represented. They may have been convinced by their lawyer that the chosen approach, though uncomfortable to them, was the only feasible one (and the lawyer may well have been right). All this is certainly not to pardon every behavior. But understanding and accepting the weakness of people under extreme pressure may at least help you not take things too personally.

31 Managing adversity

Life is not easy; being an entrepreneur even less so. Of course, some times are tougher than others. Most hardship which an entrepreneur faces is related to some kind of waste or loss. These may come in many different shapes. Time and money may be wasted on new products which do not take off. Poor financial results may force you to let go of talented and hard-working people who might have helped you turning the company around, if only you could have afforded them any longer. Prolonged legal battles may bleed you dry. Losing your most important distributor may put your whole business at risk. One of your partners turning terminally ill may cause grave material and emotional distress. The fire in your warehouse which destroys your summer collection may put your company's continuity at stake. Even if you are insured you will still be absent in the stores next season, and other brands may take your place. If a philosophical state of mind is ever required, it is when calamities occur.

Can anybody remember when the times were not hard and money not scarce?

RALPH WALDO EMERSON

Firstly about a supposedly bad over-all economic climate, as one seasoned executive puts it: 'Business is bad? So what else is new?' Times have always been tough. War has occurred throughout history. Markets have gone from boom to bust and natural disasters have struck. Hardship has always been on the menu of the human race in general and the entrepreneur more in particular. Carefree prosperity only presents itself during short intervals of time and in selected places. The good news is that the entrepreneurial species has withstood all this and still continues to survive. You as an entrepreneur may very well too, though it may be hard at times to believe it.

It is the part of an uneducated person to blame others where he himself fares ill; to blame himself is the part of one whose education has begun; to blame neither another nor his own self is the part of one whose education is already complete.

EPICTETUS

ancient Greek stoic philosopher, c. 55 - c. 135

When things go wrong, pointing the finger at others or

at yourself will make you feel both angry and powerless. Either way you will waste your energy which you need to handle the problems you're facing. The best way to deal with setbacks is to accept their being part of the package. As a result, you will keep your cool once they occur. You will not be taken aback. You will not take mishaps too personally, mistaking them for signs of some kind of unescapable bad fate pulling you downhill.

For myself I am an optimist. It does not seem to be much use being anything else.

Winston Churchill

Dealing with troubles in an impersonal manner will help you to stay confident that things will improve again sooner or later. A slight dose of optimism seems to have a nice self-fulfilling quality in practice. So apart from having a better life while working on improvement of a situation, you also increase your chances of this improvement actually happening. Statistically speaking, after having experienced a row of calamities, you would be entitled to some upside anyhow. Many companies and many businessmen have risen from what looked like their deathbed.

Prosperity is not without many fears and distastes, and adversity is not without comforts and hopes.

Francis Bacon

Not only are both triumphs and disasters of an ephemeral nature, they seldom come in the most extreme version, i.e. in full black or white. If your business does well, you may become anxious because now you have so much to lose. You may have to compromise on quality standards which were easier to maintain when your company was still small. You may also ignite new rivalry and competition. And then there are of course these rather annoying people who suddenly turn up with great ideas to improve your business even further, with great proposals to manage your retained earnings and with whatever other good or service they want to sell you.

If, on the contrary, your business does badly, you may draw new comfort from situations which you took for granted earlier on, like staff and clients wholeheartedly holding on to you in spite of rough weather. You may also be delighted by the help you possibly get from unexpected parties. At the same time, the people who buttered you up earlier on because they had to sell all these wonderful things to you, have suddenly and miraculously disappeared again. This alone can be a wonderfully liberating, mood-enhancing factor.

How do you know it's a misfortune?

Hermann Hesse

German-born Swiss poet, novelist, and painter, 1877-1962

Moreover, it may be hard to judge the total, long-term effect of events. Think of the famous Chinese Parable by Hermann Hesse. In this short story, a Chinese peasant experiences a row of fortunate events which initially appear to be curses and curses which at first appear to be fortunate events. The real consequences of the events only reveal themselves much later, if at all. They could not have been predicted, at least not at the time of their occurrence.

I neither so fawned upon nor admired another's fortune as to repent me of my own.

Marcus Tullius Cicero

ancient Roman philosopher, politician, lawyer and orator, 106 BC-43 BC

Once you're a member of the human race, you invariably tend to think that you are the only one in the world who experiences setbacks. This tendency is even stronger with entrepreneurs. Not because they are particularly hypochondriacal, but because their ways take them off the beaten track more often than others. With less direct reference available, the inclination to think your problems are unique looms large. And of course, the more unique your troubles supposedly are, the stronger your tendency to make them top of mind, whether that is helpful or not.

Just a simple question: could you mention anybody in the world with whom you would like to trade your lot? Not only his thriving business or his enviable net worth, of course, but everything. And that includes his wife, his children, his friends, his family history, his time at university. Also his health, his looks, his manners, his frustrations, his secret doubts and fears...you get the point?

I have never found that suffering improves the character. Its influence to refine and ennoble is a myth.

W. Somerset Maugham

Viewing any hardship as well-deserved and irreparable may unconsciously lead you to not doing much about it, once it occurs. This attitude may have its roots in a world view full of predestination and similar other blueprints, which supposedly set mankind up for unavoidable failure and lots of repentance rather than undertaking corrective action. Certainly in a business environment, it is better to look at adversity in a decidedly unreligious, unromantic manner. Yes, struggle builds character, but indulging in difficulties does not. Even if you have a religious or other metaphysical inclination and tend to view problems as messages from a supernatural source, try to convert these insights as soon as possible into guidelines on what to do next. Never make the mistake of settling for adversity as the default situation. Avoid telling yourself that you have deserved this. Also avoid asking yourself why you have deserved this.

He who has a 'why?' to live for can bear almost any 'how?'.

FRIEDRICH NIETZSCHE

A good way to avoid this fatalism is to have it pushed aside by the strong drive you no doubt possess to create, to produce and to succeed. If keeping your business afloat is essential to you, chances are better that you will find ways to achieve that goal. If you are normally quite resilient and at some point find yourself devoid of this power, think hard about what this tells you about your interest in your business. It is not inconceivable that you actually have wanted to call it a day for some time, waiting for some kind of minor setback to occur, which molehill is then swiftly turned into an apparently unconquerable mountain.

While the slightest inconveniences of the great are magnified into calamities, while tragedy mouths out their sufferings in all the strains of eloquence, the miseries of the poor are entirely disregarded; yet some of the lower ranks of people undergo more real hardships in one day, than those of a more exalted station suffer in their whole lives.

Oliver Goldsmith

Anglo-Irish novelist, playwright and poet, 1728-1774

No matter what your circumstances, if you are reading this book your overall situation is a privileged one. You are probably in the upper five to ten percent in terms of education and intellect in your country and in the top one percent on a global basis. Even if you are relatively poor or lonely, at least you have a well-developed mind. You are also curious, interested in getting ahead and you don't take the status quo for granted. This mental force is worth more than anything else. It is a gift which comes with obligations too, such as not exaggerating your troubles just because you happen to be able to articulate them well. Regardless of what you and your company are going through, consider yourself blessed all the same. This insight will also help you feeling obliged to do your utmost at finding your business a way out of trouble.

The average man is a conformist, accepting miseries and disasters with the stoicism of a cow standing in the rain.

Colin Wilson

English philosopher and writer, 1931-2013

While it is a good thing not to lose your head in times of calamity, you should avoid letting a detached disposition turn into a lack of decisiveness and action. If you have difficulties with creditors, approach them pro-actively with some well-considered proposals. If you see valuable staff members quit, don't hesitate to offer them a better package if they stay on. Be straight about your mistake in not having done so earlier. If your shop burns down, hunt for temporary premises to continue running your business from. Be creative. You could arrange for a shop-in-a-shop solution with another retailer or operate a mobile outlet or start offering additional web sales and delivery facilities. The show must go on, even if it's not in the way you have been accustomed to. Go the extra mile, even if it costs you more and brings in less. It will not be as costly as letting customers, suppliers or crew drift away.

Adversity is wont to disclose and prosperity to conceal the abilities of a host as well as of a general.

HORACE

Creativity and courage tend to flourish in tough situations. Tight budgets, impossible timing, extreme product requirements, extreme competitive pressure: they have a way of triggering the mind. Mankind is lazy. We need pressure to perform and whilst calamities are not the only source of pressure they certainly are an important one.

Oftentimes a reverse has but made room for more prosperous fortune. Many structures have fallen only to rise to a greater height.

LUCIUS ANNAEUS SENECA

Once you and your business have bounced back from whatever severe difficulties, you now have new confirmation that you obviously are not some kind of has-been, one-hit wonder. This happy circumstance may in turn create more confidence and a better insight into your true competencies and strengths. As a result, chances are that you will be able to put these abilities to work even more effectively. The creative ideas which emerged at gunpoint may also prove to be of value beyond the acute situation. In other words, you are all set for further growth.

One man frequently envies the prosperity of another and indulges in secret sentiments of hatred against him.

HERODOTUS
ancient Greek historian, c. 484–425 BC

There is another, somewhat cynical reason why you may find yourself back on top sooner or later after a period of serious distress. As much as people reject one-dimensional losers, they have even less liking for fellow men who seem not to have ever experienced any misery. They mistrust, envy or even outright detest flawless success stories. Once you've joined the club by having been hammered and having collected some bruises visible to the world, you will automatically meet with more sympathy, benevolence and support ever after. Whether this is a good thing or not is a different matter. It is just a law of (human) nature to acknowledge and use.

32 Success

The definition of entrepreneurial success is a highly subjective one. Creating wealth for shareholders, for associates and for oneself is probably on the agenda in most cases, given the commercial paradigm based on which business operates. But these goals, like achieving happiness or to be an ethically responsible enterprise, are too generic to be meaningful. They are by-products. Other non-money oriented criteria for success must take precedence; such as building the first good-looking e-bike, making the first silk tie which can actually be put into the washing machine or running the sushi bar with the highest customer satisfaction ratings in town. And then there are your even more personal drives which we covered earlier on. Success is what you want it to be. And what it exactly is that you want may of course change over time.

We are the doubles of those whose way
Was festal with fruits and flowers;
Body and brain we were sound as they,
But the prizes were not ours.

Robert Burton

Whenever you browse through a typical bookstore at an airport or railway station, you will inevitably see rows of cheerful motivational books with some corporate tycoon or guru with capped teeth on the cover. He or she tries to sell you some kind of magical recipe for success in business, invariably based on a true story. Just do as the hero tells you and you will supposedly be able to change your company if not your life for the better. There is one overriding problem with these success stories: you never hear from the people who have undertaken exactly the same efforts, based on exactly the same recipe, and haven't got anywhere at all. Most if not all of those war stories are anecdotal, like Freudian psychology. Their entertainment value exceeds their instructional value by a large margin.

People don't ever seem to realise that doing what's right is no guarantee against misfortune.

WILLIAM MCFEE

(English-American writer, 1881-1966)

The problem goes beyond avoiding deceptive can-do satisfaction-guaranteed literature. The real issue is that life can be plainly unfair. Doing all the right things will still not guarantee you success, entrepreneurial or otherwise, at all. The reasons for this are manifold. One is that time may just not have been on your side. You had the right ideas too soon for them to get adopted. Or you had them too late, because others before you had the same ideas but did a poor job at acting on them and spoiled the market for the next foreseeable future. But other types of bad luck may have played a role as well. What is important here is that you keep distinguishing between bad ideas or execution on your part which should make you change your approach and plain bad fortune which shouldn't. Don't change your views or lower your standards too easily. Suppose you did and the misfortune continued all the same. Then you would really have nothing left to call your own.

Man blames fate for other accidents but feels personally responsible for a hole in one.

ANONYMOUS

In psychology, this is known as the attribution theory. If I succeed it's because of me; if I fail it's because of something or somebody else. The danger of this is obvious. Irrespective of how things go, you have insufficient incentive to maintain, let alone improve your standards. If things go wrong, you won't learn from your mistakes. You will persist in making them over and over again. If things go well, you and your company will be lulled into a drowsy state of comfort. Or you will place high bets on outcomes which seem more probable than they actually are and which cannot be influenced by you or your skills, at least not to the extent that you imagine. Think of the fictional character of 007, whose invincibility supposedly even extends to the pure chance play of roulette. All good British boarding schoolboy fun of course but much less applicable to real entrepreneurial life.

Never have I trusted Fortune, even when she seemed to be offering peace; the blessings she most fondly bestowed upon me – money, office and influence – I stored all of them in a place from which she could take them back without disturbing me.

Lucius Annaeus Seneca

In order for your success to be sustainable, the safest bet is to be humble about it. Admit that luck may have played an important role in getting you where you are today and act accordingly. Prove that you have been worthy of this good fortune by raising the bar further both for yourself and for your business. Show that whether or not you may have benefited from luck so far, you certainly do not want to become dependent on it.

Failure and success seem to have been allotted to men by their stars. But they retain the power of wriggling, of fighting with their star or against it, and in the whole universe the only really interesting movement is this wriggle.

E.M. Forster

English novelist, short story writer, and essayist, 1879-1970

Fair is fair: if you as an entrepreneur (or as a human being) want to assess how successful you are, you are obliged to take into account every facilitating force which you have encountered to date. At the same time, you are allowed to consider every obstructing factor as well. It's a complex set of driving forces. First, there is your set of personal assets. The mental abilities which were or were not given to you at birth, the robustness of your health, and so on. Then there are factors such as your upbringing, your education and the over-all social and economic climate you were in. Also, consider the exchange with others which you did or did not have; the chances which did or did not present themselves to you; the investment which others have made in you; the extent to which you have maybe unjustly taken advantage of others.

Many of the same factors would then need to be applied to your venture. Which opportunities, which threats have presented themselves and how have you dealt with them? What has the competitive arena been like? Have you made the most of your assets in the broadest sense? Have you dealt with external factors honestly and effectively?

If success is to be valued in a meaningful way, all these factors must be taken into consideration. It's the only way to interpret whatever your results turn out to be.

The supreme achievement of the human spirit is to be equal to one's fortune, or live at the level of one's means.

VAUVENARGUES

Now, you may complain that it is hard work to come up with a fair appraisal of oneself and one's endeavors this way. And I agree with you. It can be done, but it's a tedious job, like a fully bespoke fitting. The only person who is able to evaluate your successes and failures over time with some accuracy is you (together, maybe, with a handful of close relatives and friends who know all there is to know about both you and your business). Only in such a concentrated, committed setting with intimate knowledge can a fair appraisal emerge.

Indeed, success, although often associated with public praise, is actually a highly individualistic affair. It is therefore better to define and enjoy it in private or with a small group of persons who are both fully informed and involved.

You have not been invited to somebody's dinner party? Of course not; for you didn't give the host the price at which he sells his dinner. He sells it for praise; he sells it for personal attention.

EPICTETUS

The prefab, generic character of universal laws of success

explains why celebrating your entrepreneurial achievements in wider circles may even feel decidedly unpleasant. It is the reason why everybody of a sound mind feels out of place when, for example, attending events where business awards of any kind are doled out. Just like gala charity dinners, they are conducted to honor the sponsors of the event, not you or your company.

Society honors its living conformists and its dead troublemakers.

MIGNON MCLAUGHLIN

This problem of feeling ill at ease with broad public acclaim may well solve itself automatically. If there is too wide a gap between your success as an entrepreneur according to your personal definition on one hand and the standards entertained by the public on the other, there will be no five star, champagne-fueled events for you to attend in the first place. Anyway, don't bother whether they materialize or not. The best way to deal with broader recognition is similar to when you are up for any badge of honor: you don't ask for it, you don't refuse it once it's granted, you don't flaunt it.

The reward of a thing well done is to have done it.

Ralph Waldo Emerson

Entrepreneurial success is actually quite simple. It is about having delivered a product or service which makes you and your workers proud, your customers delighted and your finances prosperous, without disproportional sacrifices on your part and without impairing others.

I dread success. To have succeeded is to have finished one's business on earth, like the male spider, who is killed by the female the moment he has succeeded in courtship. I like a state of continual becoming, with a goal in front and not behind.

George Bernard Shaw

A final warning on the subject. The natural by-effect of success is complacency, which may lead to decay and which may annihilate your earlier achievements. So once you have received your share of success, be a true entrepreneur and reinvest your profit, your knowledge and your personal energy in new opportunities. You might be able to breed new successes. At the very least, you will keep boredom, despair and death at bay.

33 Succession and selling the business

The life span of any human being and every undertaking is limited. Sooner or later it will be the end of the line for you and for your company as you know it. What will be the best way to capture the value inside your business and to further build it over time? What is to be your personal role in all of this, if any, as the founding owner? Are you the best man or woman to take the business to the next level, or even keep it alive in its present shape?

But though empires, like all the other works of men, have all hitherto proved mortal, yet every empire aims at immortality.

Adam Smith

If you are an entrepreneur, your business is your love child. Accept that it will grow, transform, and ultimately die – just like you. In order to prolong its life, you should try to make the business as independent from you as possible. Compare this to parents who have done a great job when the grown-up child does not need them any longer. If you succeed making yourself redundant, there will be more options to choose from when it comes to securing the company's future. You may appoint a new managing director as your successor, or hand the helm over to your children. You may merge with another company which will also take over the managerial role, transfer the business to your own senior management or sell to a third party. If you arrange to free your company from yourself, you have a better chance of being freed from your company on profitable terms.

Leaders should lead as far as they can and then vanish.
Their ashes should not choke the fire they have lit.

H.G. WELLS (ATTRIBUTED)
English writer, 1866-1946

If you decide to hold on to your company, the risk of you overstaying your welcome is considerable. In the early days of the business, you may have been a great visionary, hunter and pioneer, which is to say you have been able to create a sound business from scratch. Yet today, the company may be in need of a great farmer or store manager who is able to do maintenance and to grow it further in a steady manner. Your business may have been product-focused in the beginning. Yet today, as competition has increased, it may need to refocus on marketing. Or your business may have been a small organization with lots of improvised action and few rules and procedures. Yet today its increased size may require a higher degree of automation and more certified processes. Are you, in all honesty, still the best person to lead it?

Look at yourself in the same way you view any cost item. View it as if you were about to be employed at your company, in its present shape, for the very first time today. Would you hire yourself? Given your personal involvement, this can of course be a discomforting analysis. Time again for some straight talk with your closest supporters.

Saturninus said, 'Comrades, you have lost a good captain to make him an ill general.'

MICHEL DE MONTAIGNE

If you plan to call it a day, you need to look for a successor. Will it be somebody from within the organization? Be careful that he or she is general management material. A classic mistake is to promote people beyond the level of their abilities. The motive may be plausible: to preserve their knowledge of your company and the industry it's in, or to reward their hard work and their loyalty. But the best salesman in the world may turn out to be a mediocre commercial director. Tough as it may be for the present crew, looking outside for your successor may be the better option. If you do, make sure you make this decision palatable to the seniors who are passed over. Inform them early on about your plan and, if you would like them to stay, offer them clear tokens of your appreciation. Yes, it will cost you. But this will provide you with a safety net of loyal senior staff which can prove invaluable, also in the far from theoretical case your successor will not meet your expectations once being in the job.

To a man who has any self-respect, nothing is more degrading than to be honored, not for his own sake, but on account of the reputation of his ancestors.

PLATO

Classical Greek philosopher, writer of philosophical dialogues, mathematician and founder of the Academy in Athens, c. 427 BC - c. 347 BC

It is hard to say whether appointing your successor from your own offspring is a good idea. Odds are that it is not. Given the widely varying abilities and interests of people, it would be a mere coincidence if your son or daughter were the very best man or woman for the job. It is equally doubtful whether the job would be the ultimate self-fulfilment for him or her. Chances are that acting on your romantic ideal of preserving your empire means robbing your child of its personal destiny. Moreover, when you have several children and pick one of them as your successor, you run the risk of estranging the others no matter how careful you go about it and how much everybody seems to agree with your decision. The whole configuration of private relationships between the family members will change in any case, maybe not for the better.

Also, do not forget to consider the impact of your decisions on your other staff: a reputation for undue nepotism may repel your most talented workers. Finally, if you do decide to appoint one or more family members, allow them to do things their own way. Whatever you do, avoid monumentalizing yourself and your achievements for its own sake. Ensure that your company stays a dynamic meritocracy rather than an unworldly mausoleum.

I made my money by selling too soon.

BERNARD BARUCH (ATTRIBUTED)
American financier, stock market speculator, politician and presidential advisor, 1870-1965

Selling the business may be another alternative, of course. Consider that if a third party is ready to buy your company at a goodwill multiple of more than five times gross earnings, without obligations on your part to stay on for years for the transition, this is a fine achievement which many entrepreneurs don't reach. Do not overstretch it in terms of your asking price. Don't make the mistake of viewing the future through rose-tinted glasses. Yes, the company may grow and become more valuable. But then again, it may not. Suppose that in a couple of years, its size and profitability will have declined by, say, a third. Would you then regret having sold the business at the conditions presently offered to you?

What is a hero? Someone who has been reckless with impunity.

WILLEM FREDERIK HERMANS

Dutch novelist, essayist, polemist and physical geographer, 1921-1995

On the other hand, selling has its consequences. It is questionable whether you will ever be able again to make returns on the proceedings from the sale which are anywhere near the ones on the capital invested in your company. This is only possible if you engage in new ventures which are as risky as your current enterprise. So, unless you are offered a top dollar price by a party which is determined to conquer you for some strategic reason, selling is useful mainly when you want to reduce your risk exposure. This means preserving rather than growing your capital. In other words you stop being an entrepreneur and transform into a rent-seeker. This in turn means that in the future, you will need to put the proceedings to work in relatively safe asset classes such as treasury bills, a wide range of blue chip shares and maybe some categories of real estate.

There is no such thing as a free lunch.

Milton Friedman (attributed)

American economist, 1912-2006

Of course, this strategy will provide you with much lower returns than you have grown accustomed to. With your company, you probably make decent profits, or no party would be interested in buying you. You can spend these profits at your discretion, perhaps pocketing them yourself, and you probably also pay yourself a decent salary for good measure. Once you have sold your business, all this steady income will be gone. You will only get, say, five to seven percent annually on the cash you have been able to gain from the sale. In the current economic climate, even this modest return is hard to reach with portfolios which bear only moderate risk. To stay on the safe side, do the maths and see if you can live off three per cent per annum of the amount received. Can you afford to sell your company at all? Would you need other sources of income? What are your chances of finding them? Would you like the work involved?

Old men are fond of giving good advice to console themselves for being no longer in a position to give bad examples.

ROCHEFOUCAULD

Whatever is the best solution for you is a matter of detailed analysis which is clearly beyond the scope of this book. The best tip I can give you is to be sure to get not only detailed, but also impartial advice. A corporate finance boutique will be inclined to advise you to sell. So will a wealth manager who would love to invest the proceedings for you in stocks and bonds. A headhunter, on the contrary, will assure you that he will find you a suitable successor, so according to him there's no need to sell at all. Your accountant too will have an interest in things staying as they are, because any change of ownership or management will put his current mandate in jeopardy. Again, it is hard to get truly impartial advice because every party has its own interest. For a balanced view, you would need to talk to all of them. A more practical alternative is to get advice from a stand-alone fellow entrepreneur, possibly retired, who has gone through the motions himself, mistakes included, and who in any case does not benefit from any outcome in particular.

34 Is that all there is?

Being an entrepreneur, you have to put in more hours, mental energy and risk money than would be required in many other careers. As a result, chances are that many other aspects of life pass you by. You may be too absorbed to spend enough time with family and friends. Your lifestyle in material terms may be parsimonious for longer stretches of time. Your talent as a sculptor, cook or breeder of horses may stay undiscovered. The almost unavoidable tendency to view and exploit everything and everybody in terms of costs and benefits may narrow your mind. You may sense that your personal development is stalled. Does all this entrepreneurial activity make you a better or a worse person? What is a good person, anyway?

There are three classes of men; lovers of wisdom, lovers of honor, and lovers of gain.

PLATO

Recalling the passion for profitable results as a key characteristic of the entrepreneur, it is a safe assumption that you will at least be a lover of gain. You have to be: a selfless entrepreneur cannot exist for very long. And without at least a chance of personal gain in whatever shape, the sacrifices mentioned above would become unbearable. Moving up the ladder, you may at some point depart from this lowest, most selfish stage of development. While you may first be fixated on your own material interests full stop, you may sooner or later refocus on appraisal by yourself and others which is honor. Finally, you may fully concentrate on timeless, universal values which is wisdom.

This development is echoed in Epictetus' three stages of attributing misfortune. First you automatically blame the other, because you are self-obsessed. Your fixation on gain is a corollary of that. One step ahead you blame yourself, as a reflection of your insight that there is an outside world you need to consider and, possibly, to adapt to. Honor starts playing a role. Finally you blame nobody, because the fate of individual humans and their endeavors is largely beyond anybody's control. The best way to deal with this is to accept it, while concentrating on one's virtue as the single factor which any individual can control; and which is its own reward independent from gain or honor from others. This is when wisdom starts to emerge.

The same evolution can also be observed with regard to the law and the reasons you and I would abide by it. The psychologist Kohlberg acknowledges three main stages in this respect. At its most primitive stage, there is compliance with the law because there is a downward risk if we don't in the shape of punishment, or forfeiture of gain. On a more mature level, one complies because it is the done thing, because it pays tribute to interests of others and because it avoids social rejection i.e. loss of our personal honor. The third, most elevated viewpoint: laws are good for mankind and compliance with them is a virtue in itself. Again, no matter what it means for us in terms of gain or of honor granted by others.

The big question, therefore, is: to what extent does entrepreneurship allow, encourage or impede us to develop ourselves on the path from gain to honor and ultimately to wisdom?

Where wealth and freedom reign, contentment fails,
And honor sinks, where commerce long prevails.

OLIVER GOLDSMITH

With business being inseparably tied to gain, the next question would be: is a love of gain detrimental to obtaining honor and wisdom? It depends. A successful pursuit of gain means that you are able to make a living and do not need charity from others, which is a good thing. Furthermore, as previously discussed, your entrepreneurial gain may also entail the creation of great products and services, economic growth, employment and other positive effects for society at large. In this respect the pursuit of gain is also certainly honorable, provided that the conditions are met as we discussed them in chapter 30 (i.e. without doing outright harm to anybody or anything along the way).

As to wisdom, this is a by-product at best. It may or

may not present itself to you, while you are conducting your business and leading your life built around it. But its emerging, if at all, will always be serendipitous. The direct pursuit of wisdom in an entrepreneurial environment is futile. You may only find it when you're not looking for it.

It is possible that the scrupulously honest man may not grow rich so fast as the unscrupulous and dishonest one; but success will be of a truer kind, earned without fraud or injustice. And even though a man should for a time be unsuccessful, still he must be honest; better to lose all and save character. For character is itself a fortune.

Samuel Smiles

Acting along these lines is about as much as you can do. In business, the best attainable goal is to avoid an undue greed for gain, to stay honorable and not to bar yourself from growing wise. If this means earning a little less to live a more virtuous life, so be it. Could it mean paying your people more, charging your customers less, stepping up your product quality, avoiding deceptive advertising, cutting loose disreputable trade partners or refraining from bending the law? You are the best judge of what trade-offs apply in your situation and what choices you should make to sleep well at night.

And any occupation, art, or science which makes the body, or soul, or mind of the freeman less fit for the practice or exercise of virtue is vulgar; wherefore we call those arts vulgar which tend to deform the body, and likewise all paid employments, for they absorb and degrade the mind.

ARISTOTLE
Classical Greek philosopher and scientist, 384 – 322 BC

The possible conflicts between gain and honor are omnipresent and certainly not limited to entrepreneurial circles. Everybody who is on someone's payroll has given up some liberty of thinking, speaking and acting. Everybody who aims to earn more than what is necessary for his bare subsistence can be said to be willing to exploit his fellow men. One could argue that the higher the salary and the lower the downward risks that come with a certain position, the more degrading and corrupt that position is. Thus, entrepreneurs can be said to be more, not less honorable than many other people who work for a living.

I have known men of affairs who have made great fortunes and brought vast enterprises to prosperity, but in everything unconcerned with their business appear to be devoid even of common sense.

W. Somerset Maugham

It follows that if you are successful and happy as an entrepreneur, there is no need to pursue other interests for any ethical reason. It is, moreover, doubtful whether you would be equally successful and happy in doing so. Nature doesn't allow for extreme strengths without accompanying deficiencies in any of its species, so chances are that your strength as a businessman or -woman is offset by clear weaknesses in other departments.

At some point it may be an attractive idea to change or diversify into one or more completely different territories. You may consider going into science, becoming an actor or artist, to venture into politics or to devote your life to religion. And there are indeed examples of people who have successfully diversified or changed their occupation next to or after their life in business. But they are few and far between. It seems that entrepreneurial ability is a fairly absorbing quality which does not leave much room for other ones. That is not to say that I do not believe that you could have other interests and abilities than playing golf. It is just that these interests are unlikely to be strong enough for other than leisure deployment. By all means go out and start painting, write a thriller or study Buddhism. Just don't expect the results to be anywhere near what your entrepreneurial activity brings in.

There will be little rubs and disappointments everywhere and we are all apt to expect too much; but then, if one scheme of happiness fails, human nature turns to another; if the first calculation is wrong, we make a second better: we find comfort somewhere.

JANE AUSTEN
English novelist, 1775-1817

Sooner or later you may find that your life dedicated to entrepreneurship has become less fulfilling. If so, it's time for some careful analysis. Are you unhappy with business life as such, with the industry you're in, with the company you own, or with all three? An honest answer to this question is vital before deciding on the way forward. While quitting business altogether is always possible, you may first consider switching to another industry or looking for a different company to start up or buy.

Today as always, men fall into two groups: slaves and free men. Whoever does not have two-thirds of his day for himself, is a slave, whatever he may be: a statesman, a businessman, an official, or a scholar.

FRIEDRICH NIETZSCHE

It may well be that your concerns about your entrepreneurial existence are actually rooted in your private life. You may suddenly find that your attention is drawn to other people and other matters unrelated to your business. It may be a valuable new friendship, a love affair or an emerging passion for playing the saxophone. Or you may have family matters to address: birth, illness, death or just the dire unhappiness of anybody dear to you. Your enterprise is not to blame; any work-related obligation can be felt as hardship at times.

When I recall moments of perfect, timeless happiness [...] none of them seem to be connected with work or, indeed, any kind of striving.

JOHN CLEESE

Actually, this experience of hardship is not negative at all. Especially for the typically workaholic entrepreneur, new difficulties in dealing with the demands of the venture can be a healthy sign. It may indicate an improved consciousness of what is essential in life and what isn't.

Though it may seem odd to end this book on such a sobering note: your business is never the most important thing in your life. The intrusion of desires and needs and their apparent incompatibility with the demands your enterprise makes on you may be nothing but a wake-up call.

The most important contributor to joy and success in adult life is love (or, in theoretical terms, attachment).

GEORGE E. VAILLANT
American psychiatrist, 1934

The good news is that in the end, there may not be a need for a trade-off. As for instance the Harvard Grant Study points out, meaningful relations with others are the number one key to happiness and achievement in both private and professional life. I guess we are all well-advised to set our priorities accordingly. To ourselves through others, and to any successful enterprise through ourselves.

Thank you for having been along with me while I was writing. And once again, good luck with your enterprise.

Index

www.ingramcontent.com/pod-product-compliance
Lightning Source LLC
Chambersburg PA
CBHW030918180526
45163CB00002B/382
* 9 7 8 1 5 2 3 2 8 1 3 4 3 *